Investing for Beginners

A Fun, Practical Guide to Building Wealth and Securing Your Financial Future

Volodymyr Rybaiev

Table of Contents

Table of Contents 1
Introduction: Let's Get This Money! 3
   We've Been Sold a Lie 3
   Who's This Book For? 13
   Sneak Peek at What You're About to Learn 20
The Lowdown on Investing Basics 29
   What the Heck Is a Stock Anyway? 29
   How Do Financial Markets Really Work? 38
   What Type of Investor Are You? 44
Setting the Foundation: Your Personal Investment Plan 50
   Step One: Define Your Financial Goals 50
   Know Your Risk – Don't Sweat It, Own It 56
   Building Your Strategy Like a Pro 62
The Investment Buffet: Choosing Your Financial Weapons 69
   Stocks: The Heartbeat of the Market 69
   Bonds: Boring but Reliable 76
   What Exactly Are Funds? 87
   Real Estate: Making Bank in Bricks and Mortar 95
   Crypto: The Wild West of Investing 100
Investment Strategies That'll Make You Feel Like a Pro 111
   Passive Investing: Set It and Forget It 111
   Active Investing: Hustling in the Market 117
   Long-Term vs. Short-Term: Playing the Field 124
   Value Investing: The Warren Buffett Way 131
   Growth Investing: Riding the Rocket 137
Managing Risk Like a Boss 143

Table of Contents

Diversification: Don't Put All Your Eggs in One Basket 143
Rebalancing: Keep Your Portfolio in Check....................150
The Emotional Side of Rebalancing: Taming the Nerves 155
Investment Insurance: Protecting Your Wealth...............158
The Nitty-Gritty: Getting Started with Practical Tips 163
Opening a Brokerage Account: The First Step................163
Choosing a Broker: Who's Got Your Back? 169
Why Analyze Companies Like a Detective? 177
Analyzing Companies: Sherlock Holmes Mode 184
Conclusion: You Got This – Keep Going! 190
Wrapping It All Up..190
Motivation to Keep Crushing It..194
Bonus Sections 198
Real-Life Examples from the Big Players: Learning from the Legends...198
Charts and Graphs to Make It Visual: Numbers with Personality 204
Glossary of Terms: Because Who Doesn't Love a Cheat Sheet?...210
Exercises to Sharpen Your Skills: Keep the Momentum Rolling 218

INTRODUCTION: LET'S GET THIS MONEY!
We've Been Sold a Lie

Okay, let's get real for a second. There's this myth that's been floating around for ages—*investing is only for rich people*. You've probably heard it too. Maybe from your uncle at Thanksgiving who swears you need a boatload of cash to even think about stocks. Or maybe it's from watching movies where investment bankers are throwing down at ritzy cocktail parties, talking in numbers you can't even wrap your head around.

Here's the truth: **that's all BS.**

Yep, you don't need to be rolling in dough to get in on the investment game. In fact, investing might be the most democratic thing in finance. It's like this open-door party, and guess what? You've been invited.

So let's bust down that door and see what's really going on.

What Does It Really Mean to "Invest"?

First off, let's break down what investing actually means. It's not some *fancy-schmancy* thing where you have to wear a suit and tie and know how to read a stock ticker like a pro. Nah, investing is just **putting your money to work**.

Think of it like this: when you invest, you're basically giving your money a job. And your money, being the good little employee it is, goes out there and tries to grow. It doesn't matter if you've got $100 or $10,000. The principle is the same: you're using your money to *make* more money. And believe me, that's something anyone can do.

Let me break it down in even simpler terms. Imagine you've got a dollar. Instead of spending that dollar on a soda or a candy bar, you stick it into an investment. Maybe it's a stock, a bond, or even a real estate fund. Over time, that dollar works for you. It earns a little interest or grows in value. Next thing you know, that single dollar is worth more than when you started. That's the magic of investing, baby!

The Myth of the "Big Bucks Club"

You ever hear someone say, "I'd love to invest, but I'm not rich enough"? Yeah, I used to think that too. There's this big misconception that you need to have thousands, maybe millions, before you can start thinking about investing. But here's the reality: **that couldn't be further from the truth.**

Nowadays, you can get started with the *spare change in your pocket*. No joke. Apps like **Acorns** let you invest your *literal* spare change by rounding up your everyday purchases. Buy a coffee for $3.50? Acorns rounds it up to $4 and invests that extra 50 cents for you. Boom—you're already an investor, and you didn't even break a sweat.

And that's just the tip of the iceberg. Plenty of online platforms let you start investing with as little as $1. That's less than what you'd spend on a pack of gum. So when people tell you that you need to be rich to invest, they're living in the past, my friend. *This ain't the 1980s anymore.*

Your Money Deserves to Grow—Just Like You

Let's think about your money for a second. Right now, it's probably chilling in a savings account, earning interest that's basically less than what you'd find in your couch cushions. If that's the case, your money is being lazy. It's time to give it a new gig.

See, savings accounts are fine for keeping your money safe, but if you want it to *grow*, you need to do more. Saving is like keeping your money in a bubble. It just sits there, waiting for the day you need it. But investing? That's when your money *goes to the gym*, gets stronger, and starts working overtime for you.

And the best part? **Your money can grow no matter how much you start with.** It's all about the magic of compounding. That's when your investment earns money, and then that money earns more money, and the cycle just keeps going. It's like a snowball rolling down a hill—it starts small, but over time, it picks up speed and grows into something massive.

The Rich Got Rich by Investing—Why Shouldn't You?

Now, let me hit you with a little secret: the rich? They got rich by investing. Sure, some inherited money, others started businesses, but almost all of them *invested*. That's how the game works.

Let's take a look at **Warren Buffet**, one of the richest guys on the planet. You think he got there by stashing all his money under a mattress? Heck no! He invested. And he didn't start with a fortune either. He began investing as a kid, buying small stocks and letting them grow over time. Fast forward a few decades, and now he's one of the wealthiest dudes in the world.

You see, the rich have figured out something that too many people ignore: **your money grows faster when you invest it.** That's not just some fancy Wall Street secret—it's basic math.

And the cool part? **You don't have to be rich to do what the rich do.** You just need to start, and starting small is better than not starting at all.

Let's Talk Risk—It's Not as Scary as You Think

"Yeah, but isn't investing risky?" I can already hear you saying it. And I get it. The stock market can seem like a rollercoaster, especially if you're watching it day-to-day. But here's the deal: **there's risk in everything**, even in not investing.

Let me hit you with some truth: if you're keeping all your money in a savings account, you're actually *losing* money. Yup, you read that right. Thanks to inflation (when prices go up over time), the cash you've got sitting in a savings account is slowly losing its value. What cost you $1 today could cost $1.05 tomorrow. So, while your savings account might feel "safe," it's actually *shrinking* over time.

Investing, on the other hand, gives you a chance to outpace inflation. Yeah, there's risk, but there's also reward. And here's the thing—*you don't have to go all in*. You can start with small, low-risk investments. We'll get into the details later, but just know this: **investing doesn't have to be a gamble**. It's all about strategy.

Investing Isn't Just About Money—It's About Freedom

Now, let's flip the script for a second. We've been talking about money this whole time, but investing is about more than just dollars and cents. **It's about freedom**. It's about giving yourself options down the road. When you invest, you're not just growing your wealth—you're buying yourself choices.

You're investing in your *future*. Whether that means retiring early, traveling the world, starting a business, or just kicking back and knowing you've got enough to live comfortably. Investing is the key to unlocking those doors.

So, when you start thinking about investing, don't just see it as putting away money for a rainy day. **See it as building the life you want to live.**

You Don't Need a Suit and Tie to Play the Game

Let's address one more stereotype while we're at it: the idea that investing is only for people who wear suits and work on Wall Street. *Nope.* Investing is for anyone, anywhere. You can be wearing jeans, sipping your morning coffee, and still be an investor.

In fact, with all the tools available today—online brokerages, investing apps, robo-advisors—it's easier than ever to start investing from the comfort of your couch. You don't need a suit, you don't need an MBA, and you definitely don't need a six-figure salary to get in the game.

Start Where You Are, With What You Have

So here's the bottom line: **investing is for everyone.** You don't need to be rich, you don't need to have a ton of knowledge, and you don't need a high-paying job. You just need the willingness to start and the commitment to stick with it. Whether you've got $100 or $10,000, you can begin today.

And trust me, once you start, you'll wonder why you didn't do it sooner.

The Power of Starting Small

Let's take a minute and talk about the power of starting small. Too many people think, "I can't invest until I have a big chunk of cash." But I'm here to tell you that's nonsense. You don't need to wait until you have your life savings stacked up in a jar under your bed. You can start small—real small. In fact, the smaller you start, the better it can be for your learning curve.

Imagine you've got $50. That's it. It's what you'd spend on a night out or maybe a pair of shoes. But instead of blowing it on something temporary, what if you tossed it into an investment? You'd be surprised at how far that $50 can go. You don't need to be the next Warren Buffet overnight. **Rome wasn't built in a day, and neither is wealth.**

The real magic happens when you invest that $50, then another $50, and another. It adds up. *Trust me*—when you look back after a year or two and see how far your small investments have grown, you'll be doing a happy dance.

Consistency Is King

Here's the real secret sauce to investing: **consistency**. It's not about getting rich quick (though that would be nice, right?). It's about the slow, steady grind. We're talking long-haul stuff here.

If you invest regularly, even if it's a small amount, you're building momentum. That's where the magic of **compound interest** comes in, and if you've never heard of compound interest, let me explain it like this: it's like your money getting better at making more money.

Picture it like this: you plant a tree. It starts small, and you water it regularly. Over time, it grows bigger and stronger. But the cool part? That tree starts dropping seeds and planting more trees on its own. Soon, you've got a whole forest growing. That's what happens with your investments when you stick with it.

Don't Get Sucked Into the "Get Rich Quick" Hype

Alright, we've all seen those ads: "Make $10,000 in one week!" or "This secret strategy will make you rich overnight!" Let me stop you right there—*that's garbage*.

Yeah, sure, there are some stories of people striking it big in a short amount of time, but those are like lottery winners—super rare. And honestly? **You don't want to rely on luck when it comes to your money.** What you want is a smart, steady, reliable strategy that'll build wealth over time.

Think of investing like a marathon, not a sprint. It's about pacing yourself, keeping your eye on the finish line, and not getting distracted by the shiny things that pop up along the way. So if you ever hear someone trying to sell you on a quick money scheme, do yourself a favor and run the other way.

Investing is For the People—Like You and Me

At the end of the day, investing isn't some exclusive club for the elite. It's for regular people like you and me. Whether you're a college student scraping by on a part-time job or a single parent juggling bills, **you have the power to invest in your future.**

And here's the thing: **the sooner you start, the better off you'll be.** You don't have to wait until you've "made it" or until you've got tons of cash saved up. Start small, start now, and build from there. Because at the end of the day, investing is about creating options for yourself down the road. It's about taking control of your financial destiny.

Breaking Down the Fear

One of the biggest barriers for people when it comes to investing is fear. I get it. We've all heard the horror stories of people losing everything in the stock market crash or being taken advantage of by shady investment deals. But here's the truth: **it doesn't have to be that way.**

Yes, investing comes with risks. But so does everything in life. The key is to understand what you're getting into and to manage those risks smartly. That's what we're here for—to walk you through the basics so that when you do take the plunge, you do it with confidence.

You don't have to know everything about investing to get started. All you need is a willingness to learn and a commitment to stick with it. And the good news? There's a ton of free information out there to help you along the way (including this very book you're reading right now).

A Quick Reality Check—You Won't Become a Millionaire Overnight

Let's keep it 100 for a second. If you're diving into investing thinking you're gonna be rolling in cash by next Tuesday, I hate to break it to you, but that's not how this works. Investing is a long-term game, and it's one that rewards patience.

Will you see some gains early on? Sure, maybe. But the real magic happens over time. It's like planting a seed and watching it grow into a giant oak tree. It takes a while, but when it finally reaches full size, it's rock-solid and provides shade for years to come.

So, if you're ready to start investing, come in with the mindset that you're playing the long game. *It's a marathon, not a sprint*, and the finish line is where the real magic happens.

The Tools You Need Are Already in Your Pocket

One of the best things about investing today is that you don't need to hire a financial advisor or spend hours on the phone with a broker. You can do everything from your phone. Yeah, you heard me right. **You've got everything you need right in your pocket.**

There are apps like **Robinhood**, **Wealthfront**, **Betterment**, and **Acorns** that make investing easy and accessible for everyone. Whether you're a total newbie or you've got some experience under your belt, these apps can help you get started with just a few clicks.

You don't have to have a finance degree. You don't have to sit through boring seminars. You can start investing right now, from the comfort of your couch, with nothing more than your smartphone. So, what's stopping you?

Investing is the Ultimate Equalizer

Here's the bottom line: **investing is for everyone**. It doesn't matter where you come from, how much money you make, or what your background is. Investing is the great equalizer. It gives you the chance to take control of your financial future and build wealth over time.

So whether you're just starting out in your career or you've been grinding for years, now is the time to start thinking about investing. Not tomorrow. Not next week. **Now.**

Because the longer you wait, the more you're missing out on. And trust me, once you get started, you'll be glad you did.

Let's Wrap This Up

Alright, we've covered a lot here, but if there's one thing I want you to take away from this chapter, it's this: **investing isn't just for the rich folks. It's for you.**

You don't need to be a millionaire to start. You don't need to have piles of cash stashed away. You just need the willingness to learn, the courage to start, and the patience to see it through.

Investing is your ticket to financial freedom. It's the key to building a future where you call the shots. So, stop letting the myth that investing is only for the wealthy hold you back. You've got what it takes. Now go out there and make it happen.

Who's This Book For?

Alright, let's get real right off the bat: **who the heck is this book for?** I mean, there are a ton of books about investing out there, so why should *you* stick with this one?

If you're reading this, chances are you've already got a few questions swirling in your head. Maybe you've heard about investing from that one friend who's always talking about their stock portfolio at parties (you know the type). Or maybe you've been scrolling through Instagram, seeing people talking about "passive income" like it's the secret to life, and you're thinking, "Am I missing out on something?"

Well, spoiler alert: *yes, you are*. But don't freak out, you're not late to the game.

Let's break it down. **This book is for anyone who wants to stop being clueless about money and start getting smart about their future.**

If You're New to Investing and Have No Clue Where to Start

Let's say you're brand-new to this whole investing thing. The stock market? Sounds like a casino. Mutual funds? Is that some kind of joint bank account? Cryptocurrency? Feels like Monopoly money.

If you're feeling lost, *you're in good company*. I wrote this book *exactly for people like you*—folks who've never opened a brokerage account, who don't know what the heck an index fund is, and who are maybe just a tad bit nervous about jumping into the deep end.

And that's okay. We've all been there. The important thing is that you've recognized the need to do something with your money besides watching it sit in a savings account collecting dust. **This book is your roadmap**—no complicated jargon, no elitist Wall Street snobbery, just plain, simple advice for people who are ready to start but don't know how.

If You've Got a Little Cash But Don't Know What to Do With It

Maybe you're not entirely new to the game. You've managed to save up a little money—maybe from your job, or maybe you've been hustling on the side, and now you've got some cash that you want to *do something* with. But here's the thing: you have no idea where to put it. Stocks? Bonds? That new hotshot crypto everyone's talking about?

The options seem endless, right? It's like walking into a buffet with no idea where to start. **This book is for you**—the person who's got a little something to work with but wants to make sure they don't blow it on a bad decision.

We'll cover all the basics—where to start, how much risk to take on, and how to make smart moves without breaking a sweat. Trust me, you'll feel way more confident about where to put that money by the time we're done.

If You've Been Burned Before

Let's be honest, the world of investing can be a bit of a minefield. Maybe you've already dipped your toes into the market and gotten burned. Bought into that "hot stock" tip from your cousin only to watch it nosedive? Yeah, *we've all been there*.

If you've been burned before and you're now scared to get back in the game, I get it. I really do. But here's the thing: **you're not alone, and it's not the end of the road**. This book is here to help you dust yourself off and get back out there—*only this time, you'll be smarter about it*.

Investing is all about learning from your mistakes and making sure you don't fall for the same traps again. We'll talk about common pitfalls, how to spot bad advice from a mile away, and—most importantly—how to develop the right mindset to stay in the game long-term.

If You're Dreaming of Financial Freedom

Let's talk about dreams for a second. Everybody's got them. Some folks dream about owning a house, others about traveling the world, and a lot of us (let's be real) dream about quitting our 9-to-5 jobs and living life on our terms.

If you've ever dreamed of **financial freedom**, this book is 100% for you.

Now, I'm not going to sell you a fairy tale and tell you that investing is a fast track to quitting your job and becoming a millionaire by next week. *It's not.* But what I *will* tell you is that investing is the smartest way to start building toward that financial freedom. Little by little, step by step.

If you're willing to play the long game, to put in the time and be consistent, **investing can absolutely be your ticket to living life on your terms**. This book will show you how to start building that path to financial independence—without needing a Wall Street degree or a trust fund.

If You're Sick of Feeling Broke All the Time

We've all been there, living paycheck to paycheck, wondering why it feels like no matter how hard you work, you just can't seem to get ahead. It's like you're running on a treadmill, and the finish line keeps moving further away.

Who's This Book For?

This book is for anyone who's tired of that cycle—tired of feeling like they're always one emergency away from being flat broke. **Investing is your way out** of that grind. It's the tool you can use to stop feeling like money is controlling your life and start controlling your money.

You don't need to be rich to start investing. You just need a plan, a little know-how, and the patience to see it through. And that's what this book is all about—helping you break free from that paycheck-to-paycheck trap and start building real wealth, even if it feels impossible right now.

If You're Curious About What the Heck All the Fuss Is About

Maybe you're not even sure you want to invest yet. Maybe you've just been hearing a lot of buzz about investing and are *curious*. You're not ready to dive in headfirst, but you're willing to dip a toe in and see what all the fuss is about.

This book is still for you. We'll break down the basics in a way that doesn't feel overwhelming or confusing. By the end of this, you'll have a much better understanding of what investing is, how it works, and whether it's something you want to pursue further.

There's no pressure here. This is all about learning at your own pace and deciding what makes sense for you. Whether you decide to invest a little or a lot, at least you'll have the knowledge to make an informed decision.

If You Want to Build a Legacy

Let's zoom out for a second. Maybe you're not just thinking about yourself. Maybe you're thinking about your kids, your family, or even your community. Maybe you want to build something bigger than just a comfortable retirement. You want to build a legacy.

This book is for you too.

Investing isn't just about making money for the sake of making money. It's about creating opportunities—not just for yourself, but for the people around you. It's about building something that lasts. Something you can pass on.

Whether it's creating generational wealth for your kids or building a financial foundation that allows you to give back to your community, **investing is one of the most powerful tools you can use to create that legacy.** This book will show you how to start, how to plan, and how to think big.

If You Want to Take Control of Your Financial Future

Bottom line? This book is for anyone who's ready to stop letting life happen to them and start *taking control*. If you're tired of sitting on the sidelines, watching other people build wealth while you're just trying to make it to next month, **this book is for you**.

We'll go over the basics, dive into the nitty-gritty, and break it all down in a way that's accessible, entertaining, and—most importantly—*actionable*. Because at the end of the day, this isn't about theory. It's about taking steps toward the future you want.

Why Investing Isn't Just for the Wealthy

You might still be thinking, "Okay, but isn't investing just for rich people?" Spoiler alert: **it's not**. One of the biggest myths about investing is that you need a lot of money to get started, but that's just not true anymore. In fact, there's never been a better time to start investing with as little as $5.

For the Hustlers, the Dreamers, and the Doers

If you're someone who's always thinking about the next move, who's got that side hustle going, or who's constantly trying to figure out how to level up, **this book is for you**. You don't settle for "good enough." You're chasing *greatness*, and investing is just another way to get there.

This book isn't some boring finance lecture. It's a guide for the hustlers and dreamers who are ready to take action and do something big with their lives. You've already got the mindset—you just need the tools. And guess what? **This book has them**.

Investing Ain't a Get-Rich-Quick Scheme (But It Is a Get-Rich-Eventually Plan)

Let's just get this straight: investing isn't a magic wand. It's not some get-rich-quick scheme that'll make you a millionaire overnight. But you know what it *is*? It's a get-rich-*eventually* plan.

You're not going to see massive gains by next Tuesday, but if you play the long game—making smart, consistent moves—**you can absolutely build wealth over time**. This book is all about helping you understand the slow, steady, and ultimately rewarding journey that investing can be. We'll talk about setting realistic expectations, managing risks, and making decisions that pay off in the long run.

Still With Me? This Book's Definitely for You Then

If you've made it this far, I think it's safe to say this book's for you. Whether you're starting from scratch or you've already got a few investments under your belt, this book will give you the knowledge, confidence, and tools to take your financial future to the next level.

Who's This Book For?

Welcome to the world of investing. Let's get to work.

Sneak Peek at What You're About to Learn

Alright, let me lay it out for you: this isn't your typical boring investment guide full of stuffy, highbrow jargon that's meant to scare you off. Nah, this is gonna be **your crash course** into the world of investing, and by the time you're done with this book, you're gonna know more than half the people claiming to be "financial experts" on Twitter.

So, what can you expect from this wild ride? Buckle up, because we're about to dive into **everything** you need to know, from the basics of buying your first stock to long-term strategies for *actually* making that money work for you.

1. Why Investing Isn't Just for the Rich (and Why You Can Start Right Now)

First up, we're smashing through one of the biggest myths out there—that investing is only for the wealthy. Trust me, this whole idea that you need to be rolling in dough before you can even *think* about investing? **That's straight-up bogus**. In this chapter, I'm going to show you how you can get started with **just a few bucks**. Yep, you don't need thousands sitting in your bank account to jump into the market.

We're talking about **micro-investing** apps, low-fee brokerages, and **smart ways** to dip your toes in without feeling like you're risking it all. It's about playing the game, not about how much you start with. **Small steps still get you to the finish line**, right?

2. The Stock Market: Not as Scary as You Think

Next, we're getting cozy with **the stock market**. I know, I know. For a lot of people, the stock market seems like this

Sneak Peek at What You're About to Learn

intimidating rollercoaster that only financial wizards understand. But guess what? **It's not that deep**. At its core, the stock market is just a marketplace where people buy and sell pieces of companies, also known as stocks.

I'm going to walk you through the basics. You'll learn what a stock actually is, why prices go up and down (without needing to break out a Ph.D. in economics), and how you can use the market to your advantage. **By the end of this chapter, you'll be talking stocks like it's second nature.**

---

3. Bonds, Baby: The Safe Side of Investing

Stocks get all the glory, but bonds? **Bonds are like that steady, reliable friend who's always got your back**. If you're looking for a safe way to grow your money over time, bonds are where it's at.

In this chapter, I'm gonna show you how bonds work, why governments and companies issue them, and—most importantly—**how they can fit into your portfolio**. Think of them as the tortoise in the race. They might not move as fast, but they're solid and dependable.

---

4. Mutual Funds and ETFs: The Lazy Investor's Dream

Now, let's say you don't feel like picking individual stocks or bonds (because, let's be honest, not all of us want to watch the market every day). **Enter mutual funds and ETFs.** These bad boys are like the pre-packaged meals of investing—someone else does all the hard work of picking and choosing investments, and all you gotta do is sit back and enjoy the returns.

We'll break down how mutual funds work, how they're different from ETFs, and which one might be right for you

Sneak Peek at What You're About to Learn

depending on your goals. **The best part?** You can invest in hundreds of companies at once without lifting a finger.

5. The Art of Diversification (a.k.a. Don't Put All Your Eggs in One Basket)

You've probably heard this advice a million times: **don't put all your eggs in one basket**. When it comes to investing, this rule is golden. But how do you actually apply it? In this chapter, I'll show you how to build a **diversified portfolio**— meaning you'll spread your money across different types of investments to minimize risk.

We're talking stocks, bonds, real estate, and even *alternative* investments like crypto and commodities. The goal is to make sure that if one investment tanks, the others are there to hold you up. **It's like having a safety net for your money**.

6. Time in the Market Beats Timing the Market

Ever hear people brag about "timing the market"? Like they're some kind of Wall Street psychic who knows exactly when to buy low and sell high? Yeah, **don't listen to those folks**. Trying to time the market is a gamble at best.

What you *really* need to focus on is **time in the market**. In this chapter, we're going to explore why staying in the market long-term beats trying to predict the ups and downs. I'll show you how history proves that those who stay invested typically win out in the end. **Slow and steady wins the race**, right?

7. Dividends: Getting Paid While You Sleep

Sneak Peek at What You're About to Learn

Let's talk about one of the most *beautiful* things in investing: **dividends**. This is literally getting paid for owning stocks. Certain companies pay out a portion of their profits to shareholders, and that's called a dividend.

In this chapter, I'm going to break down how dividends work, which companies tend to offer them, and **why they can be an awesome way to build passive income**. Imagine getting a check every quarter just because you own a piece of a company. **Yeah, it's pretty sweet.**

8. Compound Interest: The Eighth Wonder of the World

Albert Einstein called **compound interest** the eighth wonder of the world, and after you read this chapter, you'll understand why. Compound interest is basically the snowball effect of money—your returns earn returns, and over time, that snowball gets *huge*.

We'll dive into how compound interest works, why it's crucial to start investing as early as possible, and how **even small contributions can grow into something massive** over time. Trust me, you're going to fall in love with compound interest.

9. Dealing with Market Crashes (Without Freaking Out)

Let's be real, markets crash. It's part of the game. But just because the market dips doesn't mean you need to freak out and sell everything. In fact, **selling during a crash is usually the worst thing you can do.**

This chapter is all about teaching you how to keep your cool when the market takes a nosedive. We'll talk about historical crashes, how the market has always bounced back, and what you can do to protect your portfolio without making knee-jerk decisions.

Sneak Peek at What You're About to Learn

10. Building Your First Portfolio (Yes, You Can Do This)

By now, you'll have a pretty good grasp on all the tools at your disposal. So, it's time to build your first portfolio. **Don't worry, I'm gonna walk you through it step by step.** We'll talk about how to choose your first investments, how to balance risk and reward, and how to set goals for both the short and long term.

I'll show you how to find the right mix of stocks, bonds, and other assets to match your risk tolerance and financial goals. **By the time you're done, you'll have a solid game plan that's built for your future.**

11. What the Heck Is a 401(k) and Why You Should Care

Retirement accounts might not be the sexiest part of investing, but they're *crazy important*. If you've got a job with a 401(k) or an IRA, congrats! You're already part of the investing world and might not even know it.

In this chapter, I'm going to break down how these retirement accounts work, why they're awesome for building wealth over time, and **how you can take full advantage of any employer matches.** Spoiler: that's basically free money, and you definitely don't want to leave it on the table.

12. Taxes: The Part We All Hate (But Gotta Deal With)

I know, I know—taxes aren't fun. But if you're gonna invest, you need to understand how taxes work. This chapter will give you a rundown of **capital gains taxes**, how dividends are taxed, and what you can do to minimize the amount Uncle Sam takes from your returns.

Sneak Peek at What You're About to Learn

But don't worry, I'll keep it light. We'll make sure you know the basics without turning this into a tax law textbook. **Promise.**

---

13. Real Estate: The Other Side of Investing

When most people think of investing, they think of stocks and bonds. But **real estate** is another powerful tool you can use to build wealth. Whether you're looking to buy a rental property or just want to understand how the housing market plays into your overall financial picture, this chapter will cover it all. We'll dive into the basics of real estate investing, how to get started even if you don't have a ton of cash, and why property can be a long-term win for your portfolio. And don't worry, you don't need to be a millionaire to get in on this. There are ways to invest in real estate that fit any budget (think REITs and house hacking—more on those later).

---

14. Crypto: What's the Deal with Digital Currencies?

You've probably heard *a lot* about cryptocurrencies by now—**Bitcoin, Ethereum**, maybe even some coins with names that sound more like memes than money. The world of crypto can be a bit wild, but it's definitely something worth paying attention to. Some people swear by it, and others say it's just a fad. So, which is it?

In this chapter, I'm going to break down the basics of crypto, explain how blockchain technology works (without boring you to death), and show you how it fits into the bigger investment picture. We'll talk about **risk, rewards**, and how to approach crypto if you're curious but not ready to bet the farm on it.

Sneak Peek at What You're About to Learn

15. Index Funds: The Set-It-and-Forget-It Strategy

If there's one thing I want you to take away from this book, it's that **investing doesn't have to be complicated**. That's where **index funds** come in. These are like the slow cooker of investments—you throw in your money, set it on low, and let it cook for years.

Index funds track a specific market index, like the S&P 500, and they're known for being low-cost, low-maintenance, and super reliable for long-term growth. In this chapter, I'll explain why **index investing** might be your best bet if you're not looking to actively manage your portfolio every day.

16. How to Stay Sane as an Investor

Investing can be an emotional rollercoaster. One day, your portfolio's flying high, and the next, it feels like the sky is falling. Staying level-headed through the ups and downs is key to long-term success.

This chapter will give you some tips and tricks to keep your cool, avoid panic selling, and **trust your strategy** even when the market gets rough. **Spoiler alert**: Most investors lose money because they let their emotions dictate their decisions. You're gonna learn how to avoid that trap.

17. Setting and Sticking to Financial Goals

What's the point of all this investing if you don't know what you're aiming for, right? In this chapter, we're going to talk about how to set **smart financial goals** that are clear, achievable, and aligned with what you want out of life.

Whether it's buying a house, retiring early, or just building a safety net, setting goals is the first step. Then, we'll talk about how to **stay on track** and adjust as you go. It's all

Sneak Peek at What You're About to Learn

about creating a plan that works for you—and sticking with it.

18. Analyzing Stocks Without Losing Your Mind

One thing that scares a lot of beginners is the idea of **analyzing stocks**. You see all these financial reports, charts, and terms like P/E ratios, and your brain just wants to check out, right? I get it.

But in this chapter, I'm going to show you how to analyze stocks in a way that's simple and straightforward. You don't need to be a math genius to figure out if a company's stock is worth buying. I'll teach you the key things to look for and how to read those reports without your eyes glazing over.

19. Rebalancing Your Portfolio: Keeping Your Investments in Check

Investing isn't just a "set it and forget it" deal (well, unless you're going full-on index funds). Every now and then, you need to **rebalance your portfolio**. This means making sure your investments still line up with your risk tolerance and financial goals.

In this chapter, I'll explain how to do that without feeling overwhelmed. We'll talk about how often you should rebalance, what to look for, and how to adjust without going overboard. It's like giving your portfolio a little tune-up every once in a while.

20. Long-Term Investing: The Ultimate Payoff

Finally, we're going to wrap things up by talking about the **big picture**. This is where all the patience and strategy pays off. Long-term investing is the key to building wealth over time—whether you're saving for retirement, a down payment on a house, or just want financial freedom.

This chapter is all about **staying the course**. You'll learn how to keep your eye on the prize, even when things get rocky. Remember, building wealth is a marathon, not a sprint. And the beauty of it? **You're in control**.

Bonus Chapter: The Power of Financial Education

Just because you finish this book doesn't mean your financial education ends here. In this bonus chapter, I'll share resources, books, and online platforms where you can keep learning and growing as an investor. **Knowledge is power**, and the more you learn, the more confident you'll become in your financial decisions.

Wrapping It Up

So, there you have it—a sneak peek at everything you're about to learn in this book. I know it seems like a lot, but trust me, we're going to take it step by step. By the time you finish, you'll be equipped with all the tools you need to start your investing journey.

And remember, investing isn't some elite club you need an invitation for. **It's for everyone**—yes, even you. So, let's get to it.

THE LOWDOWN ON INVESTING BASICS

What the Heck Is a Stock Anyway?

You've probably heard people talking about the stock market, Wall Street, or how they're "investing in stocks," but if you're new to this game, it might feel like they're speaking a completely different language. So, let's break it down in simple terms. **What the heck is a stock anyway?** And why do people keep talking about it like it's the holy grail of getting rich?

Imagine you've got this amazing business idea. You want to open up a chain of taco trucks that specialize in spicy fusion tacos. It's going to be a hit—you just know it. But here's the thing, starting up a business, especially something like a taco empire, takes cash. A lot of it. You've got to buy the trucks, stock up on ingredients, pay employees, advertise, all that jazz.

But you're not *that* rich, not yet anyway. So what do you do? You bring in some partners. You say, "Hey, if you give me some cash to get this thing rolling, I'll let you own a slice of my taco truck empire. And when it grows, and we start making some serious cheddar (pun intended), you'll get a cut of the profits."

That's what a stock is.

When a company wants to raise money, it sells off tiny pieces of itself in the form of shares, also known as stocks. So if you buy a stock, you're basically buying a little slice of that company. And when that company makes money, you might make money too. It's like you're along for the ride as that taco truck grows into a fleet.

But Why Would a Company Sell Itself Off Like That?

What the Heck Is a Stock Anyway?

Good question! Let's break it down.

Companies sell stocks for one big reason: **to raise money.** Starting a business or expanding one costs a ton of cash, and even the biggest companies in the world don't just have billions lying around. By selling shares of their company to the public, they can bring in the cash they need without having to take out loans or rack up massive debt.

For example, if a company wants to build a new factory, they can either take out a loan from a bank, which they'd eventually have to pay back with interest, or they can sell stocks to raise the money. If they sell stocks, they don't have to pay that money back. Instead, the people who buy the stocks (also called shareholders) get a piece of the pie.

So if that factory starts making the company more money, the stockholders might see the value of their shares go up, and they can sell them for a profit.

It's a win-win—the company gets cash, and the shareholders get a chance to ride the wave of success.

Okay, But What Does It Mean to "Own" a Stock?

Here's where things get a little more interesting. When you buy a stock, you actually **own** a piece of that company. It's not like owning a car or a house where you can walk up and touch it, but you are a part-owner. Congratulations, you're now a mini mogul!

Now, don't get too excited. If you buy one share of Apple, you're not suddenly going to get invited to their board meetings or have a say in how they design the next iPhone. **That's not how it works.**

But, depending on how many shares you own, you do get certain rights. For example, you might get to vote on certain company decisions, like who gets to sit on the board of directors. More importantly, if the company makes a profit, you get a share of that profit. This is called a **dividend.**

What's a Dividend, You Ask?

Ah, glad you asked! A **dividend** is kind of like a bonus check companies send to their shareholders when they're doing well. Let's go back to that taco truck empire. If your business is booming, and after paying all your expenses, you've got a bunch of cash left over, you might decide to give some of that money back to your investors. That's a dividend.

Not all companies pay dividends, though. Some companies, especially fast-growing ones like tech startups, would rather reinvest any profits back into the business to keep growing. But for some more established companies—think Coca-Cola or Procter & Gamble—dividends are a big part of why people buy the stock in the first place. It's like getting paid just for owning a slice of the pie.

So, How Do Stocks Make You Money?

There are two main ways you can make money from stocks: **capital gains** and **dividends.**

1. **Capital Gains**: This is the fancy term for when the stock's price goes up, and you sell it for more than you bought it. Let's say you bought a share of our taco truck company for $10. A year later, everyone's obsessed with spicy fusion tacos, and your company is raking in the cash. The stock price shoots up to $20. You decide to sell your share and pocket the $10 profit. Boom, that's a capital gain.
2. **Dividends**: As we mentioned, some companies pay out part of their profits to shareholders in the form of

dividends. If you own a stock that pays a dividend, you might get a check every quarter, just for holding onto the stock.

The Stock Market: The World's Biggest Auction House

Now that we've covered what a stock is, you're probably wondering, *where do people actually buy and sell these things?* Welcome to the **stock market**, my friend. Think of it like the world's biggest auction house, where stocks are bought and sold all day long.

The two biggest stock markets in the U.S. are the **New York Stock Exchange (NYSE)** and **Nasdaq**. You've probably seen the NYSE in movies—a big building with a ton of screens and a bunch of people in suits yelling at each other. That's where a lot of the trading happens. But these days, most of the stock trading is done online, so you don't need to wear a suit or shout at anyone to buy a stock.

When you buy a stock, you're not buying it directly from the company. Instead, you're buying it from someone who already owns it. And when you sell a stock, you're selling it to another investor, not back to the company. **It's a giant marketplace** where buyers and sellers come together, and the price of each stock is determined by **supply and demand**.

Why Do Stock Prices Go Up and Down?

Ah, the million-dollar question. Stock prices move up and down for all sorts of reasons, and sometimes it can feel like they're moving for no reason at all. But here's the gist: **stock prices are determined by what people think the company is worth.**

If investors think a company is going to do well—maybe they've got a hot new product coming out, or they're expanding into new markets—the demand for that stock goes up, and so does the price. On the flip side, if people think the company is in trouble—maybe they've had a bad earnings report, or a competitor is stealing market share—the demand for the stock goes down, and the price drops.

And sometimes, stock prices move because of broader market trends or even world events. If the economy is booming, stock prices tend to go up. If there's a recession, or if something big happens, like a global pandemic (sound familiar?), stock prices can tank.

The Power of Compounding: Making Money While You Sleep

One of the coolest things about investing in stocks is the power of **compounding.** This is when your money makes money, and then that money makes even more money. Let's say you invest $1,000 in a stock that grows 10% a year. After the first year, you've got $1,100. So, after the first year, your investment grew to **$1,100**. But here's where the magic of compounding kicks in: next year, that 10% growth isn't just applied to your original $1,000—it's applied to the whole $1,100. So now you're earning on top of your earnings! By the end of the second year, you've got **$1,210**. And on and on it goes.

The longer you leave your money invested, the more it grows, and it starts to feel like your money is working for you, even while you're chilling on the couch watching Netflix or catching some Z's.

But Wait—Aren't Stocks Risky?

Yup. I won't sugarcoat it—**stocks can be risky**. Unlike sticking your cash in a savings account where you know it's safe (but probably not growing much), stocks can go up **and** down. And if a company really tanks, you could lose a big chunk of what you invested.

But here's the thing: **over the long term**, the stock market has historically gone up. Sure, there are crashes—like in 2008 when the market took a nosedive—but it's always recovered. If you're patient and willing to ride out the bumps, stocks can be a great way to build wealth over time. The key is to not freak out when the market dips. It's normal. It happens. **Stay cool, keep your eyes on the long-term prize, and don't panic sell.**

Different Types of Stocks: The Risky, The Safe, and Everything In-Between

Now, not all stocks are created equal. Some are riskier than others. Here's a quick breakdown:

1. **Blue-Chip Stocks**: These are the big, established companies that have been around forever. Think **Apple, Coca-Cola, Microsoft**. These stocks are generally seen as more stable and less risky because the companies behind them are huge, profitable, and have a track record of success. You're not likely to make a quick buck with these, but they're great for **long-term investing**.

2. **Growth Stocks**: These are companies that are growing fast. They might not be profitable yet, but they've got big potential. Think **Tesla** back in the day, or tech startups. These stocks can make you a lot of money if the company blows up, but they're also riskier. If the company doesn't deliver, the stock can drop fast.

3. **Dividend Stocks**: These are stocks from companies that pay out regular dividends to shareholders. They're usually more stable companies that aren't growing super fast but generate steady profits. They're great for investors who want a regular income.

4. **Penny Stocks**: These are super cheap stocks (often under $5 a share) from small companies. They can be tempting because the price is so low, and you think, "What if this is the next big thing?" But **beware**—penny stocks are super risky and often don't pan out. You might make a quick buck, or you might lose it all.

How to Actually Buy a Stock

Alright, so now you know what a stock is and why people buy them. But how do you actually go about buying one? No, you can't just stroll into Walmart and pick one off the shelf. You need a **broker**.

A broker is like a middleman between you and the stock market. Back in the day, you'd need to call up a broker (think Wolf of Wall Street-style), but these days, it's all digital. You can open an account with an **online brokerage**—like **Robinhood, Fidelity, or Charles Schwab**—and buy stocks directly from your phone or computer.

Once you've got a brokerage account set up, you can search for the stock you want to buy, type in how many shares you want, and boom—you're in the game. Just like that, you're a stockholder.

Don't Put All Your Eggs in One Basket

Now, here's one last important thing to remember: **diversification**. That's a fancy way of saying **don't put all your money into one stock**. I don't care how hot the latest tech startup is or how much your buddy swears by his pick—investing everything into one stock is a **terrible idea**.

Why? Because if that one stock tanks, you're out of luck. But if you spread your money across different stocks (or other investments like bonds or real estate), you're reducing your risk. Think of it like this: if you're at a buffet, you wouldn't just pile your plate with mashed potatoes, right? You'd grab a little bit of everything—some steak, some veggies, maybe a slice of cheesecake. Same goes for investing.

The key to building wealth through stocks is to invest in a variety of companies across different industries. That way, if one stock takes a nosedive, your whole portfolio doesn't go down with it.

The Endgame: Financial Freedom

At the end of the day, the goal of investing in stocks is to grow your money and eventually reach **financial freedom**. Maybe you want to retire early, travel the world, or just not have to worry about money so much. Whatever your goal, investing in stocks can help you get there.

It's not an overnight thing, though. **It takes time**—and patience. You're not going to get rich quick (at least not unless you're super lucky, and let's be honest, the odds of that happening are pretty slim). But if you stick with it, keep investing, and let the power of compounding work its magic, you'll be amazed at how much your money can grow over the years.

Final Thoughts: Stock It to Me

So, now that you know what the heck a stock is, the question is: **are you ready to start investing?** The stock market can seem intimidating at first, but once you get the hang of it, it's not as complicated as it seems. It's just a matter of learning the basics, starting small, and sticking to a plan.

Don't wait. The sooner you start, the more time your money has to grow. So whether you're dreaming of owning that taco truck empire or just looking to build a nest egg for the future, stocks can help you get there.

And remember: **it's not just for the rich folks.** With today's tools and resources, anyone can start investing. So go ahead—**stock it to 'em.**

How Do Financial Markets Really Work?

Picture this: You're walking through a bustling marketplace. The air's buzzing with noise—vendors shouting, buyers bargaining, goods changing hands. Now, swap out those apples and oranges for stocks, bonds, and other fancy financial instruments, and *boom*—you've got yourself a financial market. But let's not get ahead of ourselves. We need to back up and unpack this bit by bit.

What Even Is a Financial Market?

First things first—what exactly are we talking about when we say "financial market"? Simply put, a financial market is like a big ol' marketplace where people, companies, and governments trade assets. These assets include things like **stocks**, **bonds**, **currencies**, and **commodities** (think oil, gold, etc.).

Now, you might be wondering, why do we need these markets in the first place? Well, it's kind of like why we need grocery stores. If you want to buy groceries, you don't go to ten different farms. You head to one place where everything is conveniently available. Financial markets work the same way—they bring buyers and sellers together so they can trade easily and efficiently.

The Players: Who's in This Game?

Before we jump into the nitty-gritty of how financial markets work, let's talk about the cast of characters. Because it's not just Wall Street hotshots in suits and ties (though they're definitely in the mix). Here's a breakdown of who's playing in this game:

1. **Individual Investors**: Yup, that's you and me. Anyone who buys stocks, bonds, or other assets for their own financial goals is an individual investor. Maybe you're saving for retirement, or maybe you just want to see your money grow faster than it would sitting in a

savings account. Either way, you're a player in the market.

2. **Institutional Investors**: Now we're getting into the big leagues. Institutional investors are organizations that invest large sums of money. Think pension funds, mutual funds, insurance companies, and even hedge funds (those infamous beasts). These guys have serious cash to throw around, and they can move markets with their trades.

3. **Corporations**: Companies use financial markets to raise money. Need cash to build a new factory? Issue some bonds or sell stock to investors. Corporations are always wheeling and dealing in the markets.

4. **Governments**: Believe it or not, governments are major players too. They borrow money by issuing bonds to fund everything from roads to national defense. And in case you're wondering—yes, the U.S. government is often up to its eyeballs in debt, and they use the bond market to handle it.

5. **Central Banks**: The Federal Reserve (aka the Fed) isn't just some faceless institution. It's one of the most important players in the financial world. The Fed controls interest rates, which influence the cost of borrowing money. And when they make a move, trust me, everyone pays attention.

How Do They All Play Together?

Now that you know who's in the game, how do they all interact? Think of it like a giant, global trading floor. Buyers and sellers are constantly making deals. But instead of trading physical goods, they're trading pieces of paper—or rather, digital claims to assets like stocks or bonds.

The Stock Market

The most famous of all financial markets is the stock market. When you buy a stock, you're essentially buying a piece of a company. Own a share of **Apple**, and you're technically a part-owner of that massive tech giant. Feels good, doesn't it?

But here's where things get interesting: stock prices are constantly moving up and down based on supply and demand. If more people want to buy Apple stock than sell it, the price goes up. If more people want to sell it than buy it, the price goes down. It's like an auction—prices fluctuate as people bid against each other.

The Bond Market

Now, if the stock market is like the flashy sports car of the financial world, the bond market is more like a steady, reliable minivan. Bonds are basically IOUs. When you buy a bond, you're lending money to a company or government in exchange for regular interest payments.

The bond market might not get as much hype as the stock market, but it's massive. In fact, the bond market is actually bigger than the stock market! And when bond prices shift, it can have huge ripple effects across the economy.

What Makes Markets Move?

Alright, so why do markets go up and down? Good question! Financial markets are like emotional roller coasters—they can be driven by all sorts of things, from concrete data to pure emotion. Here are a few key factors:

1. **Supply and Demand**: The most basic principle. If more people want to buy an asset than sell it, prices go up. If more people want to sell, prices go down.

2. **Economic Indicators**: Things like GDP, unemployment rates, and inflation can all move markets. If the economy is doing well, investors tend to feel more confident and buy more stocks. If it's struggling, they might sell off stocks and move to safer assets like bonds.

3. **Company Performance**: In the stock market, the performance of individual companies can have a huge impact. If a company reports strong earnings, its stock price will usually rise. If it misses expectations, the stock could plummet.

4. **Global Events**: Don't underestimate the power of world events. Wars, natural disasters, pandemics (ahem, COVID-19), and political changes can send markets into a frenzy. Investors hate uncertainty, and global events can create a lot of it.

5. **Investor Sentiment**: Believe it or not, markets can be swayed by emotion. If investors are feeling optimistic, they might keep buying stocks, even if the data doesn't fully support it. On the flip side, panic selling can cause markets to crash even if the fundamentals aren't that bad.

The Bull and the Bear: Market Moods

Speaking of emotions, let's talk about the two main moods of the market: **bullish** and **bearish**. These terms get thrown around all the time on financial news, but what do they actually mean?

- **Bull Market**: When the market is going up, and investors are feeling confident, we call it a bull market. Stocks are rising, people are making money, and everyone's feeling good.

- **Bear Market**: When the market is heading south and investors are losing confidence, we call it a bear market. Stocks are falling, people are selling, and there's a general sense of doom and gloom.

Here's a fun visual: Imagine a bull charging forward with its horns up—representing the market going up. Now picture a bear swiping down with its paws—symbolizing the market going down. There you go! Easy way to remember the difference.

Market Cycles: What Goes Up, Must Come Down

The financial markets don't move in straight lines. They go through cycles, just like the seasons. There are **boom times**, when everything's going up, and then there are **busts**, when things fall apart. It's the natural rhythm of the economy.

Booms

During a boom, everyone's making money. Stocks are rising, businesses are thriving, and people are optimistic. But beware—booms don't last forever. Eventually, things get too hot, and the bubble bursts.

Busts

A bust is the opposite of a boom. The market crashes, businesses struggle, and investors lose money. Busts can be scary, but they're also part of the game. The key is to not panic and sell everything in a rush. Remember, the market always recovers eventually.

The Role of the Federal Reserve: The Market's Puppeteer

Ah, the Federal Reserve—aka the Fed. This is one of the most important institutions in the financial world, and its decisions can make or break markets. The Fed controls **interest rates** and uses them to influence the economy.

If the Fed **lowers interest rates**, it becomes cheaper to borrow money, which can stimulate spending and investing. If the Fed **raises interest rates**, borrowing becomes more expensive, which can cool off an overheated economy.

You'll often hear financial experts talking about what the Fed is going to do next, because their decisions impact everything—from mortgage rates to credit cards, and yes, even stock prices.

Conclusion: The Market Never Sleeps

Financial markets are always on the move. They react to news, data, and even rumors. And while they might seem chaotic, they follow certain rules and cycles. Once you understand these dynamics, the whole thing becomes a lot less intimidating.

Markets can be risky, but they're also one of the most powerful tools for growing wealth over time. The key is to stay informed, stay patient, and most importantly, don't let short-term swings knock you off course.

What Type of Investor Are You?

The Risk Taker: AKA "The High Roller"

You're the kind of person who hears about a new start-up, and instead of asking, "Is this safe?" you're saying, "Where do I sign up?" You love the thrill of the game. You probably *love* the idea of hitting it big, even if it means facing some ups and downs along the way. The stock market to you is more of an adrenaline rush than a place to stash cash.

Now, don't get me wrong—being a risk-taker isn't all bad. Some of the richest folks on this planet got that way by taking some massive swings. But let's be real, it's not for everyone.

The Pros:

- Potential for *huge* returns. Think about those people who bought Apple or Amazon in the early days.
- You can stay ahead of the curve. You're probably watching tech trends, cryptocurrencies, and the next big thing in biotech like a hawk.

The Cons:

- You might end up losing big, too. If you're playing with volatile stocks, there's always the chance of a crash that wipes out a chunk of your portfolio. *Ouch*.
- The stress levels? Let's just say you might lose sleep if the market has a bad week—or a bad day, for that matter.

The Steady Eddie: AKA "The Turtle in the Race"

Slow and steady wins the race, right? You're probably the type who likes consistency. You're not out here looking for wild bets or to become an overnight millionaire. You just want a solid investment strategy that grows your wealth slowly but surely over time.

You likely invest in things like **index funds**, **bonds**, or even **blue-chip stocks**—you know, those household-name companies that have been around forever and aren't going anywhere. For you, it's all about minimizing risk and keeping your money safe while watching it grow bit by bit.

The Pros:

- You sleep like a baby. While others are biting their nails during market crashes, you're sipping tea, totally unbothered.
- Your portfolio is solid and stable. You might not see crazy returns, but you're less likely to face big losses.

The Cons:

- Your returns might be slower than you'd like. Patience is key here.
- Watching others make big gains while you're chugging along with your conservative picks can lead to a little *FOMO* (Fear of Missing Out).

The Income Lover: AKA "The Dividend Devotee"

Who doesn't like a little extra cash in their pocket? Dividend devotees are all about those regular payouts from stocks or bonds. This type of investor seeks out companies that offer dividends—a portion of the company's earnings distributed to shareholders.

Basically, instead of just hoping the stock price goes up, you're actually making some income along the way. Sounds pretty sweet, huh?

The Pros:

- You get paid regularly. Dividend payments can be like having an extra stream of income.
- These companies tend to be solid and well-established, meaning they're less likely to tank overnight.

The Cons:

- You might miss out on the high-growth companies that don't offer dividends because they reinvest profits back into growing the business.
- If the company faces tough times, they might cut those dividend payments—and that's a bummer.

The DIY Investor: AKA "The Lone Wolf"

Are you the type who loves researching stocks, analyzing balance sheets, and diving into financial news like it's a murder mystery? If so, you're probably a DIY investor. You like being hands-on with your investments, and you're not afraid to spend some time fine-tuning your portfolio.

The thrill for you is figuring out which stocks to buy, when to sell, and what sectors are about to take off. You probably *love* watching stock charts and could talk about market trends for hours.

The Pros:

- You're in control. No one's making decisions for you, and that's just how you like it.
- You're constantly learning. You get a firsthand look at how the markets work and what makes them tick.

The Cons:

- It's a lot of work. Managing your own portfolio takes time, research, and effort.

- You could make mistakes, especially if you're new to investing. A bad call could cost you more than if you had a professional guiding you.

The Hands-Off Investor: AKA "The Set-It-And-Forget-It Crowd"

If the idea of researching stocks makes your eyes glaze over, you might be a hands-off investor. You know that investing is important, but you don't want to spend your time worrying about it. That's why you might opt for things like **robo-advisors** or **target-date funds**—investments that pretty much run themselves once you put your money in.

The Pros:

- It's easy. You don't have to know much about investing to get started.
- Your portfolio is typically diversified, meaning it spreads out your risk across different types of assets (stocks, bonds, etc.).

The Cons:

- You have less control. Someone (or something) else is making the big decisions for you.
- You might not get the same kind of personalized results you would with a more active approach.

The "Fire" Investor: AKA "The Early Retiree Wannabe"

FIRE stands for **Financial Independence, Retire Early**, and if you're all about living the dream of quitting your job and retiring young, this might be you. The goal for FIRE investors is to save as much as possible as quickly as possible—often living below their means to stash away a ton of cash into investments.

These investors are super disciplined, aggressively investing in things like **low-cost index funds** or **real estate** to build wealth fast. Once they hit their "magic number" (the amount of money they need to live off for the rest of their lives), they can kiss the 9-to-5 grind goodbye.

The Pros:

- You could retire decades earlier than the average person and have the freedom to do what you want.
- You're building a huge safety net by investing smart and saving aggressively.

The Cons:

- You might have to make some serious sacrifices along the way—think cutting back on vacations, dinners out, or even buying a fancy car.
- If things don't go as planned (like a major market crash), you might have to rethink your early retirement dream.

Which Type of Investor Should You Be?

Alright, now that we've laid out the types, here's the million-dollar question: *Which one are you?* Well, that depends on a few things:

1. **Your Risk Tolerance**: Are you comfortable with seeing the value of your investments bounce around, or do you want something a little more predictable?
2. **Your Time Horizon**: How long do you have until you need the money? If you're in your 20s or 30s, you've got time to ride out market ups and downs. But if

you're nearing retirement, you might want to play it a bit safer.

3. **Your Goals**: What are you investing for? Retirement? A house? A yacht? Your goals will shape your strategy.

4. **Your Lifestyle**: How much time and energy are you willing to put into managing your investments? If you want to be hands-on, great! If not, there are plenty of ways to automate your strategy.

Mixing It Up: The Hybrid Investor

Here's a little secret: You don't have to stick to just one type. In fact, most investors are a blend of a few different styles. Maybe you have some high-risk stocks for the thrill but balance it out with bonds for stability. Or maybe you're a hands-off investor most of the time but dabble in DIY investing when something piques your interest.

It's all about finding what works for *you*. Investing isn't one-size-fits-all, and your strategy should evolve as your life and goals change.

The Endgame: Achieving Balance

Whether you're gunning for early retirement, trying to build a passive income stream, or simply want your savings to outpace inflation, figuring out your investor type is key. Once you know what makes you tick as an investor, you can tailor your strategy and watch your wealth grow.

SETTING THE FOUNDATION: YOUR PERSONAL INVESTMENT PLAN

Step One: Define Your Financial Goals

Let's get straight to it—before you can start thinking about investing, you've gotta know what the heck you're even investing *for*. Yeah, I'm talking about **goals**. You wouldn't just walk into a gym and start lifting weights without some idea of what you want to achieve, right? Same thing goes for your money. Without a goal in mind, you're just tossing cash into the wind and *hoping* it lands somewhere good. Spoiler alert: it probably won't.

So, let's break this down and figure out what your financial goals are, because that's Step One on the path to becoming the next big investing success story.

Why Setting Goals Matters

Imagine this: You're in a car, cruising along, but you have no idea where you're going. The road looks cool, but without a destination, you're just wasting gas. Your investments work the same way—without knowing where you're headed, you're just putting your hard-earned money at risk without a clear direction. And let's face it, nobody wants to end up broke because they didn't have a plan.

Setting financial goals gives your money a purpose. It's like giving it a job. You're not just saving or investing for the sake of it; you're doing it with a vision in mind, whether that's buying a house, retiring early, traveling the world, or just not being stressed every time rent's due.

Dream Big or Start Small: It's Up to You

Step One: Define Your Financial Goals

Goals don't have to be these grand, life-changing events like buying a mansion in Malibu (although if that's your vibe, go for it). They can be smaller and still super important, like building an emergency fund so that you're not scrambling the next time life throws you a curveball. Or maybe you want to save enough to finally take that dream vacation.

The point is, **your goals are personal to you**. It's all about what makes sense for your life, your situation, and your dreams. You're the driver here, so pick a destination that matters to you.

Short-Term vs. Long-Term Goals

When you're setting financial goals, it helps to break them down into two categories: **short-term** and **long-term**.

Short-Term Goals:

These are the things you want to achieve in the next few months or years. Short-term goals are like pit stops on your financial journey. They're close enough that you can almost taste them, but they still require a little planning and saving. Here are some examples:

- **Building an emergency fund**: Experts say you should have 3 to 6 months of living expenses stashed away. Yeah, I know, that sounds like a lot, but trust me, when your car breaks down or you lose your job, you'll be glad you have it.
- **Paying off credit card debt**: Those high-interest rates will bleed you dry if you're not careful. Tackling your credit card debt could save you a ton of money in the long run.
- **Saving for a vacation**: Hey, there's no shame in having fun as a financial goal! Want to head to Bali next summer? Set a number and start saving now.

Step One: Define Your Financial Goals

Long-Term Goals:

These are your bigger dreams, the stuff that's years or even decades away. They take more planning and more time, but the payoff is usually a lot sweeter. Think about these:

- **Retirement**: Whether you're dreaming of chilling on the beach at 65 or even earlier, you'll need to save a lot to live comfortably without working.
- **Buying a house**: If homeownership is part of your future plans, this is one of those long-term goals that requires serious saving.
- **College funds for the kiddos**: If you've got little ones (or plan to), thinking about their future education is a big deal. College ain't cheap, and starting to save early can give them a huge leg up.

Get Specific—Vague Goals Don't Count

"Save money" is not a goal. Neither is "Get rich." Yeah, they sound nice, but they're way too vague to be useful. To really make things happen, **your goals need to be specific**. I'm talking numbers, deadlines, and a plan of action.

Let's take "Save money" as an example. That could mean saving $50, or it could mean saving $50,000. Big difference, right? Instead, try something like, "I want to save $5,000 for an emergency fund in the next 12 months." Now *that's* a goal! It's clear, measurable, and gives you a timeline to work with.

The same goes for long-term goals. Don't just say, "I want to retire." Say, "I want to retire by 60 with $1 million saved up." That's a real target you can aim for.

The SMART Goals Formula

Step One: Define Your Financial Goals

If you want to get all fancy, you can use the **SMART goals** method. It's a popular framework for setting goals that are actually achievable. Here's how it breaks down:

- **S**pecific: Make sure your goal is clear and detailed.
- **M**easurable: You need to be able to track your progress.
- **A**ttainable: Be realistic—don't aim for something impossible.
- **R**elevant: Your goal should be important and meaningful to you.
- **T**ime-bound: Set a deadline to keep yourself on track.

For example, if your goal is to save for a down payment on a house, a SMART goal might look like this: "I want to save $20,000 in the next three years for a down payment on my first home by setting aside $555 per month." Boom, now you've got a solid plan.

Align Your Goals with Your Values

Here's a big question: **Why do you want what you want?** It's easy to get caught up in what society says you should do—buy a house, retire early, whatever—but your goals should reflect your *values*.

Are you someone who values freedom and adventure? Maybe your goal is to build up enough investments so you can travel the world full-time. Do you value security and stability? Then saving for a down payment on a home or building a killer retirement fund might be more your speed.

When your financial goals align with your personal values, you're more likely to stick with them, even when the going gets tough.

Step One: Define Your Financial Goals

Break It Down, One Step at a Time

Big goals can feel overwhelming, which is why it's super important to break them down into smaller, manageable chunks. Let's say your goal is to save $30,000 for a house in five years. Instead of freaking out over that giant number, break it down like this:

- $30,000 over five years is $6,000 per year.
- That's $500 per month.
- Which comes out to about $125 per week.

Suddenly, that big goal feels a lot more doable, right? When you break things down like this, it's easier to see how you can get there.

Write It Down (Seriously, Do It)

It's one thing to *think* about your financial goals, but it's another to actually write them down. There's something about putting pen to paper (or fingers to keyboard) that makes goals feel more real. Studies even show that people who write down their goals are more likely to achieve them.

So grab a notebook, open a Google doc, whatever—just **write down your goals**. And don't just stop there—keep track of your progress. If your goal is to save $5,000 in a year, check in every few months and see how close you are. If you're falling behind, adjust your plan. If you're ahead of the game, congrats!

The Power of Visualization

Here's where it gets a little woo-woo, but stick with me. **Visualizing your goals** can actually help you achieve them.

Picture yourself living the life you want. What does it look like? How do you feel? Where are you? What are you doing?

By creating a mental image of your future self, you give your brain something to work towards. It's like you're setting the GPS for your life. The clearer the vision, the easier it is to make decisions today that move you toward that future.

Stay Flexible—Life Happens

I hate to break it to you, but life doesn't always go according to plan. You might lose a job, have a surprise expense pop up, or maybe your priorities change along the way. That's totally okay. The key is to stay flexible and **adjust your goals when needed**.

Just because you hit a bump in the road doesn't mean you should throw in the towel. Maybe you need to extend your timeline, lower your savings target, or change your focus altogether. The important thing is to keep moving forward, even if it's at a slower pace.

Know Your Risk – Don't Sweat It, Own It

Alright, let's talk about **risk**. I know, the word alone might make your palms a little sweaty, but here's the deal: **risk is a part of life**. You take risks every single day, whether you're aware of it or not. From deciding to jaywalk across the street to ordering that questionable-looking sushi at the gas station (yeah, we've all been there), life's full of unknowns. But when it comes to your investments, you don't have to be scared of risk—you can learn to *own it*.

Let's break it down. We're gonna talk about why risk is something you should embrace, not fear, and how you can *smartly* manage it so you don't end up having a full-blown panic attack every time the stock market has a bad day.

What Exactly Is Risk?

When you hear "risk," you probably think of something negative. Like, "Oh no, risk! That means I'm gonna lose all my money and end up living in a cardboard box!" But that's not the full story. Risk, when we're talking about investing, simply means there's a chance things won't go the way you planned. It's uncertainty.

Let's say you're driving to work, and there's a *chance* you'll hit traffic. That's a risk. Does it stop you from driving? Nope. You get in the car, maybe leave a little earlier, and get on with your day. Same goes for investing.

Risk is the price of entry when it comes to investing. You're putting your money into the market, and you're hoping it grows. But there's always a chance it won't. Stocks could tank, the economy could hit a rough patch, or some company you invested in might go belly-up. That's the risk you take. But don't panic—because there are ways to manage it.

Why You Can't Avoid Risk (And Why That's Okay)

Here's a truth bomb: **You can't avoid risk entirely.** No matter how much research you do, no matter how safe you try to play it, there's always going to be some level of risk involved in investing. And you know what? That's a good thing.

Why? Because **without risk, there's no reward**. If you just stash your money under your mattress, sure, it's safe from the stock market's ups and downs, but it's not growing either. And let's be real, thanks to inflation, that money is actually losing value over time. So, in a way, *not* investing is also a risk!

The key is to **embrace risk**. Don't let it scare you away from investing altogether. Instead, let it empower you. By understanding risk, you'll be better equipped to handle the highs and lows and make smart decisions with your money.

Different Types of Investment Risks

Not all risks are created equal, my friend. There are a few different types you should be aware of when it comes to investing. Understanding these will help you figure out how much risk you're willing to take on and how to navigate it without breaking a sweat.

Market Risk

This is the big one everyone talks about. **Market risk** refers to the chance that the entire stock market could go down. When the economy takes a hit, when there's political uncertainty, or even when a global event (like, say, a pandemic) happens, the market could dip or even crash. It's the risk you sign up for when you invest in the stock market.

Credit Risk

Also known as **default risk**, this is the risk that a company or government you've lent money to (through buying bonds) won't be able to pay you back. If a company goes bankrupt, for example, they might default on their bonds, leaving you with a loss.

Interest Rate Risk

This is mostly for bond investors. If you're invested in bonds and interest rates go up, the value of your bonds could go down. It's just one of those weird quirks of the bond market that you've got to be aware of.

Liquidity Risk

This is the risk that you won't be able to sell your investment when you want to. Let's say you've got money tied up in a real estate investment. If the market is slow and you need to sell quickly, you might have trouble finding a buyer, and you could end up having to sell for less than it's worth. That's liquidity risk.

So, How Much Risk Can You Handle?

Now, this is where things get personal. **Your risk tolerance** is how much risk you're comfortable taking on without losing sleep at night. Some people are adrenaline junkies—they thrive on the rollercoaster ride of high-risk, high-reward investments. Others are more like, "I'll take the scenic route, please."

How do you figure out your risk tolerance? Start by asking yourself a few key questions:

- **How much can you afford to lose?** If you're investing your emergency fund in stocks, slow your roll. That's money you might need in the short term, and you don't want to risk it on a volatile investment. If you're investing for retirement 30 years down the line, you can afford to take on more risk.

- **How do you handle stress?** If the thought of losing 10% of your portfolio in a market downturn makes you want to puke, you probably have a lower risk tolerance. That's okay! You can still invest, but you'll want to stick to safer options.

- **What's your timeline?** The longer you have until you need your money, the more risk you can take on. If you're investing for a short-term goal, like buying a house in two years, you'll want to play it safe.

Risk vs. Reward—Finding the Balance

Investing is all about **balancing risk and reward**. High-risk investments have the potential for high returns, but they also come with a higher chance of losing money. Low-risk investments, on the other hand, are safer but won't grow your money as fast.

Here's a basic rule of thumb: **The younger you are, the more risk you can afford to take on.** If you're in your 20s or 30s, you've got decades ahead of you to ride out the ups and downs of the market. That means you can afford to invest in riskier assets like stocks, which have the potential for higher returns over time.

As you get closer to retirement or other big financial goals, you'll want to **dial back the risk** and shift more of your money into safer investments like bonds or even cash. This way, you protect the gains you've made and ensure that your money is there when you need it.

Diversification: Your Secret Weapon

One of the best ways to manage risk is through **diversification**. This is just a fancy way of saying, "Don't put all your eggs in one basket." By spreading your money across different types of investments—stocks, bonds, real estate, etc.—you reduce the risk that a loss in one area will tank your entire portfolio.

Think about it like this: If you're only invested in tech stocks and the tech sector crashes, you're in big trouble. But if you're also invested in bonds, real estate, or even international markets, those other investments can help offset your losses.

Don't Be Afraid to Take Calculated Risks

Look, investing isn't about playing it totally safe. If you want to grow your wealth, you'll need to take some **calculated risks**. This means doing your homework, knowing what you're getting into, and being okay with the fact that not everything is going to be a winner.

It's like that saying, "No risk, no reward." If you're willing to take a little risk and ride out the rough patches, you'll come out ahead in the long run.

Handling the Emotional Side of Risk

Investing isn't just about numbers; it's also about **managing your emotions**. Watching the stock market take a nosedive can be terrifying, especially if you've got a lot of money invested. But here's the thing: **Panicking is the worst thing you can do**.

When the market drops, a lot of people freak out and sell their investments, locking in their losses. But smart investors stay calm and ride out the storm. In fact, market downturns can be a great opportunity to buy more stocks at a lower price. It's all about having a long-term mindset.

Remember: **The market is going to fluctuate**. That's just how it works. If you're in it for the long haul, those ups and downs will even out over time.

The Bottom Line: Own Your Risk

At the end of the day, you can't avoid risk, but you can **own it**. By understanding the different types of risks, figuring out your personal risk tolerance, and diversifying your investments, you can confidently navigate the ups and downs of the market.

Investing is a journey, and like any journey, there will be bumps along the way. But if you stay cool, calm, and collected, you'll reach your destination with more money in your pocket than when you started. So don't sweat the risks—**embrace them**. After all, no great story ever started with someone playing it safe.

Building Your Strategy Like a Pro

Alright, so you've learned the basics about investing, you've wrapped your head around risk, and you're probably wondering, *what's next?* Well, this is the fun part. Now, it's time to **build your strategy**. Yep, it's time to go from a regular ol' investor to an investor with a **game plan**. And trust me, you don't need to be a Wall Street pro to do this. You just need to know how to mix a little knowledge with some confidence.

This chapter is going to take you through the process of **building an investment strategy**—one that works for you. We're going to break it down step by step, so you don't get lost in the jargon or feel like you're being force-fed financial advice you'll never actually use.

Why You Need a Strategy (Hint: It's Not Optional)

Here's the deal: **investing without a strategy is like driving without a map.** Sure, you might get lucky and stumble onto the right path, but chances are, you're just gonna get lost. A solid strategy keeps you focused, helps you make better decisions, and keeps you from freaking out the moment things don't go exactly as planned (because trust me, they won't).

So, what exactly is a strategy? In simple terms, it's your roadmap. It's a plan that outlines *how* you're going to invest, *where* you're going to invest, and *why* you're investing in the first place. It's what keeps you from going all-in on that "hot stock tip" your cousin's friend's brother told you about at the barbecue last summer.

Here's why a strategy is non-negotiable:

- **Keeps you grounded.** You won't get swayed by the latest market trends or panic every time the stock market dips.
- **Guides your decisions.** With a clear plan, you'll know exactly when to buy, when to sell, and when to just chill.
- **Helps you stay focused on your goals.** Investing is a marathon, not a sprint. A strategy keeps you from chasing after quick wins that might sabotage your long-term goals.

Step 1: Set Clear, Realistic Goals

Alright, so let's start at square one: **What do you want out of this?**

Your strategy starts with **your goals**. And I'm not talking about vague, wishy-washy goals like, "I want to be rich!"—no, we're talking concrete, specific goals. What are you trying to achieve by investing? Are you saving for retirement? Trying to build a down payment for a house? Maybe you want to start your own business in five years. **Whatever it is, get specific.**

Break it down like this:

- **Short-term goals**: These are things you want to achieve in the next 1-5 years. Think: saving for a wedding, a vacation, or an emergency fund.
- **Mid-term goals**: These are goals you want to hit in the next 5-10 years. Maybe it's a down payment on a home or building up a nest egg for your kid's college.

- **Long-term goals**: This is the big one—your retirement fund, or building serious wealth over time. Think 10 years and beyond.

Why do goals matter so much? Because different goals require different investment strategies. If you need your money in a year or two, you're not going to invest it in high-risk stocks. But if you've got decades to grow your wealth, you can afford to take on more risk.

Step 2: Figure Out Your Risk Tolerance

Remember when we talked about risk in the last chapter? Well, this is where that comes into play. **Your risk tolerance** will shape your strategy. Some folks are all about those high-risk, high-reward moves, while others want to keep things slow and steady.

To figure out where you stand, ask yourself:

- **How much risk are you comfortable with?**
- **How much time do you have before you need to cash out your investments?**
- **How would you feel if your portfolio lost 10%, 20%, or even 30% in a single year?**

Be honest with yourself here. There's no right or wrong answer—just what's right for *you*. If you can't sleep at night because you're worried about market volatility, then a lower-risk strategy is probably your jam. But if you're young, and you've got time to recover from losses, you might be able to handle more risk.

Step 3: Choose Your Asset Allocation

Alright, so here's where we get into the nitty-gritty. **Asset allocation** is a fancy way of saying, "How are you going to divide up your money between different types of investments?"

There are three main asset classes to consider:

1. **Stocks**: The most popular option for growing wealth over the long term. Stocks are risky, but they offer high returns if you're in it for the long haul.
2. **Bonds**: These are safer and more stable than stocks. Bonds pay you interest, but they generally offer lower returns.
3. **Cash and cash equivalents**: Think savings accounts, money market accounts, and CDs. Super safe, but also super low returns.

Your asset allocation is going to depend on two things: **your goals** and **your risk tolerance**. If you're saving for retirement and you've got decades to go, you might go heavy on stocks—like 80% stocks, 20% bonds. But if you're older, or your goals are more short-term, you might go more conservative—like 60% stocks, 40% bonds or even 50/50.

Pro Tip: Asset allocation is not a set-it-and-forget-it thing. You're going to want to rebalance your portfolio from time to time to make sure it still lines up with your goals and risk tolerance.

Step 4: Diversify, Diversify, Diversify

This step can't be overstated enough. **Diversification** is like the golden rule of investing. It's what keeps you from putting all your eggs in one basket and then watching helplessly as that basket gets stomped on by the stock market.

When you diversify, you spread your investments across different asset classes, industries, and even geographic regions. That way, if one area of your portfolio tanks, you've got other investments to pick up the slack.

How to diversify like a pro:

- **Across asset classes**: Don't just invest in stocks. Have some bonds and cash in the mix too.
- **Within asset classes**: Don't put all your money in tech stocks. Get a mix of industries—tech, healthcare, energy, consumer goods, etc.
- **Globally**: Don't just invest in U.S. stocks. Consider adding international stocks to your portfolio to get exposure to other markets.

Pro Tip: One of the easiest ways to diversify is by investing in **mutual funds** or **ETFs**. These funds pool money from a bunch of investors to buy a diverse range of stocks, bonds, or other securities. It's like buying a pre-made smoothie instead of chopping up all the fruits yourself.

Step 5: Stay Consistent and Stick to the Plan

Once you've built your strategy, the key is to **stick to it**. It's easy to get caught up in the day-to-day fluctuations of the market and start second-guessing your plan. But remember: **investing is a long game**.

You're not in this to make a quick buck—you're in it to grow your wealth over time. That means not freaking out every time the stock market takes a dip, and not getting overly excited every time it shoots up.

Stay the course. You've built a strategy based on your goals, risk tolerance, and timeline, and that strategy is designed to withstand the ups and downs. Trust it.

Step 6: Keep Learning and Adjusting

Here's a little secret: even the pros are always learning. **Investing isn't a one-and-done thing.** Markets change, new opportunities pop up, and your personal goals might evolve. That's why it's important to **keep learning** and be open to making adjustments along the way.

- **Keep an eye on your portfolio.** Check in every few months to see how things are going. Are you on track to hit your goals? Does your asset allocation still fit your risk tolerance?

- **Rebalance when necessary.** If your asset allocation has shifted too far in one direction (for example, if your stocks have done really well and now make up 90% of your portfolio), it might be time to rebalance. That means selling some of your over-performing assets and buying more of the underperformers to get back to your original allocation.

- **Stay curious.** There's always something new to learn when it comes to investing. Whether it's exploring new asset classes, learning about ESG (Environmental, Social, and Governance) investing, or just keeping up with the latest market trends, the more you know, the better you can fine-tune your strategy.

Building Wealth Like a Pro

By now, you've got the tools you need to build an investing strategy like a pro. It doesn't have to be complicated, and you don't need to be some Wall Street genius to make it work.

It's all about **setting clear goals, understanding your risk tolerance**, and **diversifying your investments**. With these key ingredients, you'll be well on your way to building wealth and achieving financial independence.

And hey, if you ever start to doubt yourself, just remember: **even the best investors started right where you are now**. The important thing is to get started and keep learning as you go.

THE INVESTMENT BUFFET: CHOOSING YOUR FINANCIAL WEAPONS

Stocks: The Heartbeat of the Market

Let's get one thing straight right off the bat: **stocks are the bread and butter of investing**. They're the sexy, headline-grabbing, roller-coaster-ride financial tools that make the world of investing so exciting. But for a lot of folks, the stock market feels like this **mysterious, high-stakes casino** where the rules don't make any sense unless you've got an MBA and a Bloomberg terminal. Spoiler alert: **it's not that complicated**.

In this chapter, we're diving into the world of stocks—how they work, why they're important, and how you can ride the stock market waves without getting seasick. We're gonna break it all down, *no fancy finance speak*, and give you the lowdown in a way that makes sense for *you*, no matter how much—or how little—you know about stocks.

So, What Exactly Is a Stock, Anyway?

Alright, let's start with the basics: **what the heck is a stock?**

At its core, a stock is a tiny piece of ownership in a company. When you buy a share of stock, you're buying a **sliver of that company's pie**. Own a share of Apple? Congrats, you're now a part-owner of one of the biggest companies in the world. You don't get to stroll into headquarters and start bossing people around, but you do get a say in certain things—like voting on company decisions—and, more importantly, you get to share in the company's **profits** (if they make any).

Stocks are like the heartbeat of the market. They pulse with the health of the economy, the buzz around tech innovation, and the rumors swirling on Wall Street. They reflect how people feel about the companies they represent and, by extension, how people feel about the future.

In simple terms:

- **Stock = Ownership.**
- **Price goes up = You're making money.**
- **Price goes down = You're losing money (but not necessarily for good).**

It's really that straightforward. Now, let's dig deeper.

How Stocks Are Born: The IPO Story

Ever heard someone talk about an "IPO" like it's the hottest ticket in town? That's because it kind of is. IPO stands for **Initial Public Offering**, and it's when a company first sells its shares to the public. It's like when a business decides to take off its training wheels and ride into the stock market.

Here's how it goes down:

1. A company—let's say it's a hip new tech startup—has been privately owned for a while. The founders and early investors own all the shares.
2. The company wants to raise money to grow (maybe they want to build new products, expand into other countries, or buy that cool office building downtown).
3. So, they **go public**—meaning they sell shares to regular ol' people like you and me.
4. Boom, the stock is listed on a stock exchange, like the New York Stock Exchange (NYSE) or NASDAQ, and people can start buying and selling.

The day a company goes public is like a **coming-out party for stocks**. It's often a big, flashy event with headlines, media hype, and sometimes insane price swings. But after the IPO buzz wears off, the stock settles into the daily grind of market life, where its price is determined by *supply and demand*.

Why Do Stock Prices Go Up and Down?

Alright, let's talk about what everyone really wants to know: **why do stock prices change?** And let's be real—sometimes they change *a lot*.

The stock market is like this living, breathing thing. Prices go up and down every day based on **investor emotions, news, and company performance**. Sometimes it's logical, sometimes it's not (looking at you, GameStop).

Here's a breakdown of the big factors that move stock prices:

- **Company Performance**: This is the big one. If a company's killing it—making more money than expected, launching popular products, or beating out the competition—its stock price tends to go up. On the flip side, if a company misses earnings expectations or faces a scandal, the stock price can tank.

- **News & Events**: Stocks live and die by the headlines. Bad news—like a CEO scandal, layoffs, or poor sales—can make investors hit the "sell" button fast. On the flip side, positive news—like a big merger or a new product launch—can send stocks soaring.

- **Investor Sentiment**: Sometimes, it's all about the **vibe**. If investors feel confident about the future, they're more likely to buy stocks. If they're scared (say, there's a recession looming or a global crisis), they might panic and start selling. This can create huge swings in stock prices, even when nothing fundamental about the company has changed.

- **Supply and Demand**: It's Economics 101—when more people want to buy a stock than sell it, the price goes up. When more people want to sell than buy, the price goes down.

How Do You Make Money with Stocks?

Alright, now for the fun part—**making money**. There are two main ways to make dough with stocks:

1. **Capital Gains**: This is the most obvious way. You buy a stock for, say, $50, and it goes up to $100. Congrats, you've just doubled your money. When you sell that stock, you "realize" those gains (fancy finance speak for *you cash out*).

2. **Dividends**: Some companies pay out part of their profits to shareholders in the form of dividends. Think of it like a little bonus check just for owning the stock. Dividends are usually paid out quarterly, and while they're not guaranteed, they can be a nice income stream, especially if you own a lot of shares in dividend-paying companies.

But here's the catch—**stock prices can go down too**. If you buy a stock at $50 and it drops to $30, you've lost money *on paper*. You don't actually lock in that loss until you sell the stock. That's why a lot of seasoned investors preach **holding onto stocks long-term**—because over time, the market generally trends up, and many of those short-term losses can be recovered.

The Two Types of Stocks: Common vs. Preferred

Not all stocks are created equal. There are **two main types of stocks** you can own:

- **Common Stock**: This is what most people are talking about when they say "stocks." Common stock gives you ownership in the company, voting rights, and the potential for dividends. However, if the company goes belly-up, common stockholders are last in line to get paid (if they get paid at all).

- **Preferred Stock**: This is a bit different. Preferred stockholders get paid **before** common stockholders if the company issues dividends or goes under. They also get fixed dividends, so there's less upside (no voting rights and usually no massive gains if the stock price skyrockets). Think of preferred stock as a cross between a stock and a bond.

Stocks vs. Other Investments: Why They're So Popular

So, you might be wondering, **why are stocks such a big deal?** Why not just invest in something "safe" like bonds or real estate?

Here's the thing: **stocks offer the highest potential return** over the long term. Historically, the stock market has returned around **7-10% per year**. Sure, some years it's a bloodbath, and others it's a total gold rush, but over time, stocks have outperformed just about every other type of investment.

That's why even though they're riskier, **stocks are the go-to choice for people looking to build wealth.**

Stocks also offer something that a lot of other investments don't: **liquidity**. If you need cash fast, you can sell stocks in a matter of seconds (not always a great idea, but the option is there). Try doing that with real estate or bonds—it's not nearly as easy.

How to Pick Stocks (Without Losing Your Shirt)

Now, let's get to the part where most people freeze up: **picking the right stocks**. This is where things can feel overwhelming because there are thousands of stocks out there, and they're not all created equal.

The key to picking stocks isn't about finding the next Apple or Tesla (though if you do, props to you!). It's about **doing your homework** and **investing in solid, fundamentally strong companies**. Here are a few things to look for:

- **Revenue and Earnings Growth**: You want to invest in companies that are growing, right? Look at their financial statements (I know, it sounds boring, but it's important). Are their revenues and profits increasing year over year? If a company is making more money, that's usually a good sign.

- **Price-to-Earnings (P/E) Ratio**: This is a quick way to see if a stock is overpriced or undervalued. A lower P/E ratio might mean the stock is undervalued (and could be a good buy), while a higher P/E ratio could mean it's overvalued.

- **Debt Levels**: How much debt is the company carrying? Too much debt can be a red flag, especially if the company isn't making enough money to pay it off.

- **Competitive Advantage**: Does the company have something that sets it apart from its competitors? Maybe it's a killer brand (like Nike), a unique product (like Tesla), or a huge market share (like Amazon). Look for companies with a **moat**—a competitive edge that keeps the competition at bay.

The Power of Diversification: Don't Put All Your Eggs in One Basket

If there's one golden rule in investing, it's this: **don't put all your eggs in one basket**. Translation: **don't invest all your money in one stock**.

Sure, you might be tempted to go all-in on that hot new tech company your buddy told you about, but that's a risky move. Instead, spread your money across different stocks, sectors, and even asset classes.

Diversification helps protect you from losing your shirt if one of your stocks tanks. If you're invested in 20 different companies, a loss in one won't ruin your whole portfolio. It's like having backup singers—if one's off-key, the show can still go on.

Long-Term vs. Short-Term Investing: Playing the Stock Game Smart

One of the biggest mistakes new investors make is thinking they need to **get rich quick**. They see stories of people who turned $10,000 into $1 million in a few months and think that's the norm. Spoiler alert: **it's not**.

The stock market rewards **patience**.

Bonds: Boring but Reliable

Alright, let's get something out of the way first. **Bonds don't exactly scream "excitement,"** do they? I mean, when was the last time you heard someone brag at a party about their bond portfolio? Yeah, that's what I thought. But here's the thing: **bonds may not be the most thrilling investment on the planet**, but what they lack in drama, they more than make up for in stability and reliability.

You know that saying, "slow and steady wins the race"? That's basically bonds in a nutshell. They're like the dependable, **boring friend** who shows up to help you move. You might not invite them to your wild weekend plans, but when life gets tricky, you're glad they're around. Let's dig in, and I promise, by the end of this chapter, you might just see why **bonds are the backbone** of any solid investment portfolio.

What Even Is a Bond?

Let's start with the basics—**what the heck is a bond, anyway?**

A bond is essentially a **loan you give to a government, corporation, or other entity.** Think of it this way: they need money, and instead of going to the bank, they go to you (and a bunch of other investors) to borrow it. In return, they agree to pay you back with interest over time. It's like when your buddy borrows twenty bucks but promises to pay you back with a little extra for your trouble.

So, in simple terms:

- **You = The lender.**
- **The government or company = The borrower.**
- **The bond = The IOU with interest.**

Unlike stocks, where you're buying a piece of ownership in a company, **with bonds, you're the creditor**. If things go south, bondholders get paid before stockholders (more on that later), which makes bonds a *safer bet* than stocks.

How Do Bonds Actually Work?

Bonds work on a pretty simple premise: **you lend money, you get paid back**. Here's how it breaks down:

1. **You buy a bond**—say, a government bond for $1,000.
2. **You hold onto that bond** for a set period of time (let's say 10 years), and during that time, the bond issuer (like Uncle Sam) pays you interest every six months.
3. **At the end of those 10 years**, the bond "matures," and the issuer pays you back your original $1,000, plus all the interest you earned along the way.

It's like a little money machine that just chugs along in the background, pumping out interest payments without much drama. And unlike stocks, which can soar to the moon or crash into the ground, **bonds are pretty chill**. You know exactly how much you're going to earn and when you're going to get paid.

The Appeal of Bonds: Stability & Safety

Now, why would anyone want to invest in bonds when there are more exciting options out there? One word: **stability**.

When the stock market is on a wild roller-coaster ride (as it often is), **bonds are like the calming, Zen master** in your portfolio. They offer a steady stream of income and—most importantly—they **protect your money**. When you invest in bonds, especially government bonds, the chances of losing your initial investment are pretty slim. That's why people refer to them as "safe-haven" investments.

Let's face it, sometimes the stock market feels like it's out to give you a heart attack. But with bonds, you can sleep easy knowing that you've got **something reliable in your corner**. Sure, you're not going to double your money overnight, but you're also not going to lose your shirt in a market crash. **Slow and steady, remember?**

Types of Bonds: Not All Are Created Equal

Alright, so not all bonds are the same. **There are a few different flavors** to choose from, and they all have their own quirks. Here's a quick breakdown of the main types:

1. Government Bonds (Treasuries)

These are the **gold standard of bonds**—safe, secure, and backed by the good ol' U.S. government. When you buy a U.S. Treasury bond, you're essentially lending money to Uncle Sam, who has a pretty solid track record of paying people back.

- **Treasury Bills (T-bills)**: Short-term bonds that mature in one year or less.

- **Treasury Notes (T-notes)**: Mid-term bonds that mature in 2 to 10 years.

- **Treasury Bonds (T-bonds)**: Long-term bonds that mature in 20 to 30 years.

Government bonds are considered **about as safe as it gets**, which is why retirees, conservative investors, and anyone looking to protect their nest egg often flock to them. The downside? **They don't pay a ton of interest**. You're trading higher returns for peace of mind.

2. Corporate Bonds

Corporate bonds are a bit riskier than government bonds, but they also offer higher returns. When a company needs to raise money, they might issue bonds to do so. As the investor, you're lending money to the company in exchange for regular interest payments.

The thing with corporate bonds is that not all companies are created equal. You've got big, stable companies like **Apple or Microsoft**, whose bonds are pretty safe. But you've also got smaller or struggling companies that might offer higher interest rates but come with a lot more risk.

In the bond world, **higher risk means higher reward**. But be careful—investing in corporate bonds from companies with shaky financials could end up biting you if they go belly-up.

3. Municipal Bonds (Munis)

Municipal bonds are issued by cities, states, or other local government entities. These bonds are often used to fund public projects like schools, highways, and hospitals. One big perk of munis is that they're usually **tax-exempt**, meaning you don't have to pay federal taxes on the interest you earn. Sometimes, they're even exempt from state and local taxes, too.

So, if you're looking to keep more of your investment income, **munis can be a smart choice**—especially if you live in a state with high taxes.

4. Junk Bonds

Now, this is where things get interesting. **Junk bonds** are basically corporate bonds on steroids. These are bonds issued by companies with shaky credit or high debt levels. Because they're riskier, they offer **juicy interest rates** to attract investors.

The trade-off? You could make a lot of money... or you could lose it all if the company defaults. That's why they call them "junk" bonds—it's a high-risk, high-reward game, and not for the faint of heart. But if you've got an appetite for risk, junk bonds could be worth a look.

How Bonds Fit Into Your Investment Portfolio

So, why should you care about bonds when stocks are clearly the superstar of the investment world? Well, **bonds and stocks are like the yin and yang of investing**. They balance each other out. While stocks offer the potential for huge gains, they also come with the potential for huge losses. Bonds, on the other hand, are the safety net that keeps your portfolio grounded.

Think of it like this: **if stocks are the thrill-seeking adventurer, bonds are the cautious planner**. You need both to build a well-rounded portfolio. **Diversification** is the name of the game here. By having a mix of stocks and bonds, you can protect yourself from the wild swings of the stock market while still earning a solid return over time.

Here's a quick rule of thumb: **the older you get, the more bonds you should own**. Why? Because as you get closer to retirement, you want to lock in your gains and protect your money from market volatility. Stocks can be unpredictable, but bonds? **They're as steady as a rock.**

Why Do Bond Prices Change?

Alright, here's a little curveball: even though bonds are considered "safe," their **prices can still fluctuate**. Why? The biggest reason is **interest rates**.

Here's how it works: let's say you buy a bond that pays 3% interest. If interest rates rise and new bonds are issued at 5%, suddenly your 3% bond isn't looking so hot. As a result, the price of your bond might go down if you try to sell it before it matures. On the flip side, if interest rates fall, your bond becomes more attractive, and its price might go up.

So, while bonds are generally more stable than stocks, **they're not immune to price changes**. But if you hold your bond until it matures, you'll get your full principal back, plus the interest you were promised. That's why bonds are often seen as a **long-term investment**—you lock in your return and don't have to worry about day-to-day price swings.

The Role of Inflation

Inflation is like the sneaky villain in the bond world. **It quietly erodes your purchasing power** over time. Here's the deal: if inflation rises, the value of your bond's fixed interest payments goes down in real terms.

For example, let's say you own a bond that pays 4% interest, but inflation is running at 3%. That means your **real return** is only 1%. It's like running on a treadmill—you're moving, but you're not really getting anywhere.

This is why some investors look for **inflation-protected bonds**, like **Treasury Inflation-Protected Securities (TIPS)**. These bonds are designed to keep pace with inflation, so your purchasing power stays intact, no matter what.

Conclusion: Boring, But Beautiful

So, yeah, **bonds might be the boring sibling of stocks**, but sometimes boring is exactly what you need. They're reliable, predictable, and they **help you sleep at night**—especially when the stock market feels like a rollercoaster.

Whether you're looking to diversify your portfolio, protect your wealth, or just add a little stability to your financial life, bonds are an essential piece of the puzzle. They may not make headlines or give you a rush of adrenaline, but in the end, they're the unsung heroes of the investment world.

Bonds vs. Stocks: Why You Need Both

At this point, you might be thinking, "Okay, bonds sound fine, but I'm really more into stocks—should I even bother with bonds?" **Short answer: Yes. Long answer: Absolutely, yes.**

Here's the deal—**stocks and bonds complement each other** like peanut butter and jelly. They have different purposes, and when you combine them in the right proportions, you're creating a balanced meal for your investment portfolio. Stocks give you the potential for high returns, while bonds provide stability and a cushion against volatility.

It's a classic case of risk vs. reward:

- **Stocks**: High risk, high reward.
- **Bonds**: Low risk, lower reward, but with a higher chance of getting what you expect.

By holding both, you're **hedging your bets.** When stocks are soaring, you're riding the wave. But if things go south, your bonds are there to keep things steady. It's like wearing a seatbelt in a car—you're still enjoying the ride, but if things get bumpy, you're protected.

The Ideal Bond Allocation

Now, the big question: **how much of your portfolio should you allocate to bonds?**

This is where things get personal. **Your age, risk tolerance, and financial goals all come into play.** A popular rule of thumb is the **"100 minus your age" rule**: subtract your age from 100, and that's the percentage of your portfolio that should be in stocks, with the rest in bonds.

So, if you're 30 years old, 70% of your portfolio could be in stocks, and 30% in bonds. By the time you're 60, the balance shifts to 40% stocks and 60% bonds. The idea is that as you get older and closer to retirement, **you want more of your money in safer investments, like bonds,** and less in volatile stocks.

But rules of thumb are just that—**rules of thumb.** Your specific situation might call for a different approach. Maybe you're more conservative and want a higher percentage of bonds early on. Or maybe you're more of a risk-taker and want to keep more in stocks longer. **It's all about finding the right balance for you.**

A Few Bond Myths—Busted!

Let's clear up a couple of misconceptions about bonds while we're at it. Because while they're straightforward, **bonds often get misunderstood.**

Myth #1: Bonds Are Only for Retirees

Sure, **bonds are a favorite among retirees** because they offer stability and a steady income stream. But that doesn't mean they're only for people sipping piña coladas on a beach. Bonds are a great investment for anyone who wants to diversify and protect their portfolio. If you're saving for a big purchase—like a house or your kid's college education—bonds can be a safer way to grow your money without taking on too much risk.

Myth #2: Bonds Don't Offer Good Returns

Yes, bonds typically offer lower returns than stocks, but they're also much less risky. And here's the kicker: **over the long term, bonds can actually outperform stocks, especially during periods of economic uncertainty.** While stocks can crash and burn, bonds keep plugging along, providing consistent, if not flashy, returns.

Myth #3: Bonds Are Complicated

Nope. While the jargon can sometimes make it seem like you need a PhD to understand bonds, the concept is actually pretty simple. **You lend money, you get paid back with interest.** That's it. Sure, there are different types of bonds and different risk levels, but at the end of the day, bonds are one of the most straightforward investments out there.

Riding Out Market Storms with Bonds

Here's something to keep in mind: **the economy moves in cycles.** Sometimes stocks are on fire, and everyone's making money hand over fist. Other times, the market takes a nosedive, and people panic.

Bonds are your **financial life jacket** in these situations. They don't completely remove the risk, but they'll keep you afloat when stocks are sinking. During market downturns, bonds tend to hold their value better than stocks, and in some cases, **they might even go up in price** as investors flee to safer assets. That's why bonds are often called a "flight to safety."

When things are good, it's easy to get caught up in the excitement and **forget about the boring bonds** sitting in the corner. But when the market turns ugly, that's when you'll be glad you had them. Bonds are like the trusty insurance policy you hope you never have to use, but when you do, you're thankful it's there.

Bond Funds: An Easier Way to Invest

Okay, by now you're probably thinking, "Do I really have to research individual bonds? That sounds like a lot of work." The good news? **You don't.**

Bond funds make it easy to invest in bonds without having to hand-pick each one. These funds pool money from a bunch of investors (including you) and use that money to buy a mix of bonds. By investing in a bond fund, you're getting instant diversification and professional management.

There are **all kinds of bond funds** out there, from government bond funds to corporate bond funds to high-yield (junk) bond funds. Some funds focus on short-term bonds, while others invest in long-term bonds. You can pick a bond fund that matches your investment goals and risk tolerance without having to sift through hundreds of individual bonds yourself.

The Final Word: Bonds Deserve Respect

Let's be real—**bonds will probably never be the stars of the investment world**. They're the humble, behind-the-scenes worker bees that get the job done without making a fuss. But that doesn't mean they don't deserve your respect.

In fact, if you're serious about building a well-rounded investment portfolio that can weather the ups and downs of the market, **bonds should be a key part of your strategy**. They offer stability, income, and protection from volatility—things that every investor needs, no matter how young or old.

Bonds: Boring but Reliable

So, next time someone tells you that bonds are boring, just smile and nod. Because deep down, **you'll know the truth: boring can be beautiful.**

The end.

4o

Вы сказали:

Write Funds: The Easy Button for Diversification. Written for an American audience. Written in a lively, informal style. Written in the style of an essay or a novella. Written in simple language, accessible to a wide range of readers, but at the same time rich and expressive. Many colloquial expressions and slang are used, creating an atmosphere of lively speech. Structure your text for easier reading. Highlight phrases, paragraphs in ways that are accessible to you, for optimization and ease of reading. Chapter has at least 30000 words. If you encounter a character limit, DO an ABRUPT stop, and I will send a "continue" as a new message. If the chapter is finished, write "The end". Before writing your answer, rate it on a 10-point scale according to the following criteria: interesting plot, meaning, interesting thoughts, dynamism, author's style, imagery, desire to finish reading, general impression. If the score is below 10 points, correct your answer and then write. Each chapter has at least 30000 words.

ChatGPT сказал:

ChatGPT

Alright, let's dive into **funds**—the investment world's ultimate "Easy Button." And no, I'm not just talking about some magic solution that'll instantly make you a billionaire. But in the crazy world of investing, where there are too many choices, funds are as close as you can get to an all-in-one deal.

What Exactly Are Funds?

If stocks and bonds are like choosing individual songs from a playlist, **funds** are like hitting "shuffle all." A **fund** is essentially a basket full of investments—stocks, bonds, or even both—that someone else picks for you. You buy a slice of that basket, and *boom*, you're instantly diversified across a bunch of companies, industries, or even countries.

So, instead of stressing over which specific stocks or bonds to buy, funds do the heavy lifting for you. **You don't have to be a financial genius to invest in them.** Just hit that "Easy Button" and let someone else handle the fine print.

Mutual Funds vs. ETFs: Two Sides of the Same Coin

Now, when it comes to **funds**, there are two main flavors: **mutual funds** and **ETFs** (Exchange-Traded Funds). They're pretty similar, but like Coke vs. Pepsi, each has its own vibe. Let's break it down real quick:

Mutual Funds: The Classic Option

- With mutual funds, you buy into a pool of investments, and **a fund manager does the buying and selling** for you.
- You don't trade these on the stock exchange like stocks. Instead, they're priced once a day, usually at the end of the trading day.
- You typically need a minimum amount of money to get started, which can be a couple hundred bucks or more.

Mutual funds are like going to a sit-down restaurant: you order, the chef (fund manager) cooks it up, and you enjoy the meal when it's ready.

What Exactly Are Funds?

ETFs: The New Kid on the Block

- ETFs, on the other hand, trade like a stock. You can buy and sell them throughout the day, just like you would with any stock on the exchange.
- There's no minimum investment. If you've got the cash to buy one share, you're in!
- They tend to have lower fees than mutual funds, because most of them are **passively managed**—meaning no fund manager is calling the shots. They just track a market index, like the **S&P 500**.

ETFs are more like grabbing a meal at a food truck—**quick, flexible, and easy on the wallet.**

Diversification 101: Don't Put All Your Eggs in One Basket

Okay, so why is everyone always going on about **diversification**? It's because diversification is basically **the golden rule of investing**. It's all about **spreading your risk**. You don't want to bet all your money on one horse, or in this case, one stock.

Let's say you only own stock in one company, and that company tanks. Guess what? You're stuck riding that ship down. But if you own a fund that invests in a hundred different companies, and one of them tanks? **No sweat**—you've still got 99 others keeping you afloat.

Diversification means **spreading your investments across different types of assets** (stocks, bonds, real estate, etc.) and across different sectors (technology, healthcare, energy, etc.). **Funds do this for you,** giving you a pre-packaged way to lower your risk without having to become an expert in every single industry out there.

The Benefits of Hitting the Easy Button with Funds

Still not convinced? Let's talk about why funds are so dang popular:

1. Instant Diversification

With funds, you're **not putting all your eggs in one basket**. You're getting a little bit of everything—tech, healthcare, consumer goods, whatever the fund focuses on. It's like building a team of all-star players instead of betting on just one person to carry the game.

2. Managed by the Pros

When you invest in a mutual fund, there's typically **a professional fund manager** making decisions on your behalf. These guys and gals spend their days knee-deep in financial data, trying to squeeze out every bit of performance they can. So, if you don't feel like becoming a stock market expert, **let the pros handle it**.

3. Less Stress, More Chill

Keeping up with individual stocks is a lot of work. You'd have to read quarterly earnings reports, track market trends, and stay on top of the news. With funds, all you have to do is pick a good one, set it, and forget it. **It's stress-free investing** for people who've got better things to do than stare at stock charts all day.

4. Flexible Options

There's a fund for everything. **Want exposure to clean energy? There's a fund for that.** Interested in global stocks? You guessed it—there's a fund for that too. Whether you're conservative and want mostly bonds or aggressive and looking for high-growth stocks, **there's a fund to match your goals**.

5. Cost Efficiency

What Exactly Are Funds?

One of the best things about ETFs is that they often have **lower fees** than mutual funds. Why? Because many ETFs are **passively managed**, meaning they just track a market index rather than having a manager picking and choosing stocks. Lower fees = **more of your money stays in your pocket**.

Common Types of Funds: Something for Everyone

Just like there are different kinds of ice cream, there are different flavors of funds. **Pick your favorite, or mix and match!**

Index Funds

These are **the OG of passive investing.** Index funds track a specific index, like the S&P 500, and **own all the companies in that index**. They don't try to beat the market—they just try to match it. These funds are popular because they tend to have **lower fees** and they've historically performed well over time.

Warren Buffett himself is a huge fan of index funds. **If it's good enough for him, it's probably worth looking into.**

Sector Funds

Sector funds focus on a specific part of the market—think tech stocks, healthcare, energy, etc. They're a great way to target your investments if you have a hunch that a certain industry is about to take off.

Just keep in mind: **sector funds are more volatile** because they're concentrated in one area. But if you're feeling bold, these can give you the potential for higher returns.

Bond Funds

If you're looking for **stability**, bond funds might be your jam. These funds invest in bonds rather than stocks, providing **a**

steady income stream without the rollercoaster ride of the stock market. Perfect if you're more of a risk-averse type.

International Funds

Want to go global with your investments? **International funds** invest in companies outside of the U.S., giving you exposure to markets that might not be as tied to the American economy. It's a great way to **diversify geographically**, but be aware that foreign markets can sometimes be a bit unpredictable.

Fees, Fees, Fees: What You Need to Know

Before you hit the "buy" button on any fund, there's something important you need to look at: **fees.** Every fund charges fees, but they can vary a lot from one to the next. **The lower the fees, the more money you keep in your pocket.**

Expense Ratio

The most important fee to look at is the **expense ratio.** This is the annual cost of owning the fund, expressed as a percentage of your investment. So, if the expense ratio is 0.50%, you're paying $5 a year for every $1,000 invested.

A low expense ratio is good—**anything under 0.50% is solid.** ETFs usually have lower expense ratios than mutual funds, which is one reason why ETFs have exploded in popularity.

Other Fees to Watch Out For

Some funds charge **sales loads**—basically, a commission you pay when you buy or sell shares. **Avoid these if you can.** Why pay extra when there are plenty of no-load funds out there?

Choosing the Right Fund for You

Alright, now that you know the basics, **how do you pick the right fund?** It all comes down to your goals and your risk tolerance.

1. Know Your Goals

Are you saving for retirement? A house? Just trying to grow your wealth? Your goals will help you decide what type of fund is right for you. If you're young and have a long time before you need the money, you can afford to be more aggressive with **stock-heavy funds**. If you're nearing retirement, you'll probably want more **bonds and conservative investments**.

2. Assess Your Risk Tolerance

How much can you stomach seeing your investments go up and down? If market volatility freaks you out, stick with **lower-risk funds** like bond funds or conservative balanced funds. If you've got a strong stomach for risk, go for **growth funds** or **sector funds**.

Timing the Market: Don't Even Try

One of the biggest mistakes investors make is trying to **time the market**—basically, trying to guess when the market is going to go up or down and adjusting your investments accordingly. Here's the truth: **nobody can predict the market, not even the pros**. Trying to time the market is a recipe for stress and disappointment.

Instead, the key to successful investing is to stay in the market **long-term** and **stay consistent**. Put your money in, leave it alone, and let time work its magic. **The market goes up and down**, but over the long haul, it has historically gone up. So, trying to time every dip and peak? That's like trying

What Exactly Are Funds?

to predict the weather for your beach vacation three months from now. **Just don't bother.**

Dollar-Cost Averaging: The No-Stress Way to Invest

If timing the market is out, what's in? **Dollar-cost averaging (DCA).** It sounds fancy, but it's just a straightforward strategy where you invest **a fixed amount of money at regular intervals**, regardless of what's happening in the market.

The beauty of DCA is that it takes all the guesswork out of investing. **You don't have to worry about whether the market is up, down, or sideways**—you just keep buying. Over time, this smooths out the highs and lows, giving you an average price for your investments. It's like grabbing stuff on sale when prices drop and paying a bit more when they go up, but in the end, it all evens out.

Plus, DCA is a great way to make investing **a habit.** You're not waiting for the "perfect" moment—you're just consistently building your portfolio one step at a time.

The Role of Rebalancing: Keep Your Portfolio on Track

Okay, so you've got your fund(s), you're dollar-cost averaging like a boss, and now you're thinking, "Do I just set it and forget it?" Not quite. **Every so often, you'll want to check in on your portfolio** to make sure it's still aligned with your goals. This is where **rebalancing** comes in.

Let's say your ideal mix is 70% stocks and 30% bonds. Over time, if stocks have a great year, you might find your portfolio has shifted to 80% stocks and 20% bonds. That's when you need to rebalance—**basically, sell off some of your winners and buy more of your laggards** to get back to your original mix.

Rebalancing keeps your risk in check and ensures you're not overexposed to any one type of asset. Plus, it's a sneaky way of following the old investment adage: **buy low, sell high.** You're selling the assets that have done well and buying the ones that haven't—at least, not yet.

Funds: The Easy Button with a Few Extra Perks

By now, you're probably starting to see why funds are such a solid option for beginner investors and seasoned pros alike. **They give you instant diversification, professional management, and low stress.** What's not to love? But there's one more thing that makes funds stand out: **they can be customized to fit your lifestyle.**

Maybe you're a tech geek and want to invest in cutting-edge innovations, or perhaps you're all about sustainability and want your money to go into eco-friendly companies. Whatever your vibe, there's probably a fund out there that aligns with your values. From **socially responsible funds** to **target-date retirement funds**, you can find one that suits both your financial goals and your personal beliefs.

The Bottom Line: Funds are Your Best Friend in the Market

Here's the deal: **investing doesn't have to be complicated.** Funds are the ultimate Easy Button, offering diversification, simplicity, and flexibility all in one neat package. Whether you're all about playing it safe with bonds or ready to take on the world with growth stocks, there's a fund that'll fit you like a glove.

So don't stress about picking individual stocks or trying to predict the next market crash. Just hit that Easy Button, find a fund that works for you, and start building your future—one consistent investment at a time. **You've got this.**

Real Estate: Making Bank in Bricks and Mortar

Alright, buckle up, because we're diving into the world of **real estate investing**, a land of endless opportunity, where "flipping" isn't just for pancakes, and "location, location, location" is more than just a cliché. In this chapter, we're getting down to the nitty-gritty of **how real estate can seriously level up your financial game**—whether you're dreaming of owning your first rental property or fantasizing about living off the rent checks like some real estate mogul.

But, let's not kid ourselves: real estate is no get-rich-quick scheme. There's work involved, some risk, and maybe even a bit of luck. But if you play your cards right, you can be **making bank from bricks and mortar** in ways you never imagined.

Why Real Estate Rocks (And Why You Should Care)

You might be thinking, "Why real estate? I'm already overwhelmed with stocks, bonds, and all this other investing mumbo-jumbo." Well, let me tell you—real estate isn't just **another investment option**. It's like having a **superpower** in your back pocket. The difference? Real estate is **tangible**. You can touch it, walk through it, and even live in it (not the case with your stock portfolio).

Here's why real estate deserves a spot in your financial strategy:

- **Steady cash flow**: You get monthly rent checks. Enough said, right?
- **Appreciation**: Over time, real estate tends to **increase in value**.
- **Leverage**: You can buy real estate with **other people's money** (hello, mortgage!).

- **Tax benefits**: From deductions to depreciation, the tax code is basically **in love** with real estate investors.

The best part? You don't need a trust fund or a Wall Street office to get started. With the right mindset, a little knowledge, and maybe a touch of hustle, **you can jump into real estate and start making serious moves.**

Cash Flow: Your Monthly Money Machine

Let's start with the best part of real estate investing—**cash flow**. Think of it as the steady stream of **income** that flows into your pocket every month, courtesy of your tenants. Unlike stocks, where you're crossing your fingers for dividends, real estate lets you create **predictable, steady income** if you do it right.

Imagine this: You buy a duplex, rent out both units, and—after covering all expenses like the mortgage, taxes, and maintenance—you've got a few hundred bucks left over each month. That's **cash flow**. Now imagine owning ten properties like that. Yeah, we're talking real money now.

Pro tip: If you want to make sure your properties are cash-flow positive, do your homework. Don't just buy any house and hope it works out. Look at **rental demand, local property values**, and **expected expenses**. A solid property will bring in more income than it costs to operate.

Appreciation: Making Money While You Sleep

Okay, so cash flow is the immediate benefit, but let's not forget about **appreciation**—the long game in real estate. **Appreciation** is the increase in the value of your property over time. Buy a house today for $250k, and in ten years, it might be worth $400k. That's a nice little nest egg without you lifting a finger.

And while we're at it, let's clear up a myth: **You don't have to buy in an up-and-coming neighborhood** to make money from appreciation. Sure, buying in a "hot" area might accelerate your returns, but even regular ol' neighborhoods can see **significant value increases** over time.

The trick is to **stay in the game long enough**. Real estate isn't a quick flip (well, unless flipping's your thing—more on that later). It's about patience, persistence, and letting time do the heavy lifting. **Real estate is a marathon, not a sprint.**

Leverage: The Power of Using Other People's Money

One of the most incredible things about real estate is that you can use **other people's money**—aka **leverage**—to build wealth. Let's break it down:

In most cases, when you buy stocks, you pay for the entire stock upfront. But with real estate? You can buy a property with just a **down payment**—usually around 20%—and the rest is covered by a mortgage. This means that for a $300,000 property, you might only need to fork over $60,000.

But here's where the magic happens. When your property appreciates in value, you get the benefit of that increase **on the entire property value**, not just your down payment. So, if your $300k property appreciates by 10%, you gain $30,000 in equity—even though you only initially invested $60k. That's the **power of leverage**.

Of course, leverage is a double-edged sword. If the property value drops, you could be stuck owing more on your mortgage than the property's worth (that's called being **underwater**), so make sure you're smart about how much debt you take on.

The Many Ways to Play the Real Estate Game

So, you're sold on real estate, but where do you start? The good news is, there are **multiple ways to get into real estate investing**, depending on your budget, skills, and goals.

Here's a quick rundown of your options:

1. Rental Properties

The most common and straightforward path. Buy a property, rent it out, and collect rent checks every month. This could be anything from a **single-family home** to a **multi-unit apartment building**. Just make sure the rent covers your mortgage and expenses (and leaves you with some profit).

2. House Hacking

If you're just starting out and don't have a ton of cash, house hacking might be your best bet. The idea is simple: you buy a property, live in one part of it, and rent out the rest. For example, buy a **duplex**, live in one unit, and rent out the other. The rent can help cover your mortgage, letting you **live for cheap**—or even for free.

3. Flipping

For the risk-takers and go-getters, **flipping houses** can be a lucrative game. You buy a property that's undervalued, fix it up, and then sell it for a profit. The key here is speed—**the faster you can flip it, the better your return**. But beware, flipping can also be a lot of work and stress, not to mention a hefty dose of risk if you don't know what you're doing.

4. Real Estate Investment Trusts (REITs)

If you love the idea of real estate but don't want the hassle of being a landlord, consider **REITs**. These are companies that own, operate, or finance real estate and pay out most of their profits to investors in the form of dividends. Think of it like owning stock in a real estate company. **It's passive, diversified, and doesn't require you to manage anything.**

5. Commercial Real Estate

If you want to step things up a notch, you can venture into **commercial real estate**—think office buildings, retail spaces, and warehouses. The potential for cash flow is higher than residential properties, but so is the risk. Commercial tenants tend to sign **longer leases**, which means more stability, but these investments typically require more capital upfront.

The Risks: Don't Gloss Over Them

We'd be doing you a disservice if we didn't talk about the **risks**. Real estate, like any investment, isn't without its downsides. **Property values can drop, tenants can bail on rent, and unexpected expenses can pile up** faster than you can say "new roof." So, make sure you've got some cushion in your budget and an emergency fund to cover the unpredictable.

The good news is, with a little planning and research, you can manage most of these risks. Being informed and proactive is your **best defense**.

The Long Game: Building Wealth Over Time

Real estate investing is all about **building long-term wealth**. If you're in it for the quick buck, you might want to rethink your strategy. But if you're willing to **stick it out** and let time work its magic, you can accumulate serious wealth, thanks to the trifecta of **cash flow, appreciation, and leverage**.

Crypto: The Wild West of Investing

Welcome to the Wild West, partner. No, not the one with cowboys, shootouts, and tumbleweeds—though it might feel that way at times. I'm talking about the **crazy, chaotic, and downright exhilarating** world of **cryptocurrency**. It's an arena where fortunes can be made (and lost) faster than you can say "blockchain."

And here's the thing: **crypto** isn't for the faint of heart. If you're the type who likes your investments neat, tidy, and predictable, then maybe this chapter isn't for you. But if you've got a wild side, a dash of adventurous spirit, and a curiosity about **how digital money is shaking up the world**, then grab your cowboy hat and saddle up. It's time to ride.

What Even Is Crypto? (And Why Should You Care?)

Let's start with the basics, 'cause I'm guessing you didn't come here for a PhD-level lecture on cryptography. In its simplest form, **cryptocurrency is digital money**—currency that exists only in electronic form. No paper bills, no coins, just **1s and 0s floating in cyberspace**. But unlike the dollars in your bank account, crypto isn't controlled by any government or central bank. Instead, it's decentralized, which means it operates on a **network of computers** (fancy term: blockchain).

Now, before your eyes glaze over, here's the part that matters to you as an investor: **crypto is volatile**. We're talking massive price swings that make the stock market look like a kiddie pool. And while that kind of volatility might scare off traditional investors, for some, it's exactly what makes **crypto the wildest, most exciting game in town**.

The Rise of Bitcoin: The OG of Crypto

If we're gonna talk about crypto, we've gotta start with the **granddaddy of them all—Bitcoin**. Back in 2009, some mysterious figure (or group) known only as **Satoshi Nakamoto** created Bitcoin as a new form of digital currency. The idea? To create a peer-to-peer system for transactions without needing a bank or government to oversee it. No middleman, just you and the other person, sending money digitally through the magic of **blockchain technology**.

For a while, Bitcoin was the kind of thing you'd hear about from your weird cousin who's always ahead of the curve on internet trends. But fast-forward a few years, and Bitcoin is now a **household name**, with mainstream investors, celebrities, and even governments talking about it.

Why? Because people started making **ridiculous amounts of money** with it. Folks who bought Bitcoin for a few bucks in the early days woke up to find their investment worth millions. Naturally, that got a lot of attention.

The Great Crypto Gold Rush: Why Everyone's Jumping In

Let's face it: nobody likes to miss out on a **get-rich-quick opportunity**. And when Bitcoin started surging, it kicked off what you might call the **Great Crypto Gold Rush**. Suddenly, there were more cryptocurrencies popping up than Starbucks on a city block.

From **Ethereum** and **Dogecoin** to **Solana** and **Cardano**, each new coin came with its own promises of being the next big thing. Some of them lived up to the hype, while others? Well, they're more like those old-timey snake oil salesmen—full of promises but with nothing to back them up.

Here's the kicker, though: it's not just about **currency** anymore. Cryptocurrencies have evolved into **an entire**

ecosystem, with use cases far beyond just sending and receiving money. You've got **smart contracts, DeFi (Decentralized Finance), NFTs (Non-Fungible Tokens)**, and so much more. Crypto has become **the tech frontier** where innovation meets finance, art, gaming, and even real estate. Wild, right?

The Pros and Cons: Should You Take the Plunge?

So, why should you care about crypto as an investor? The answer depends on how much of a **risk-taker** you are. Let's break it down:

Pros:

- **Insane potential returns**: We're talking 100x returns in a short span if you hit it right. The kind of gains you **dream about**.
- **Decentralization**: No government, no central bank. Crypto is **all about power to the people**.
- **Cutting-edge tech**: You're not just investing in currency. You're buying into a whole new financial ecosystem.
- **Diversification**: Crypto adds a whole new dimension to your portfolio that you just won't get from stocks and bonds.

Cons:

- **Volatility**: Crypto can **skyrocket one day and tank the next**. If you can't handle wild price swings, it's not for you.
- **Risk of loss**: Many cryptos have gone belly up, leaving investors with nothing.

- **Regulatory uncertainty**: Governments are still trying to figure out what to do with crypto, and that could affect its future.
- **Security risks**: You've probably heard about crypto exchanges getting hacked and people losing millions. Yeah, that's a thing.

Bottom line? **Crypto isn't for the faint-hearted.** It's risky, unpredictable, and sometimes downright stressful. But if you're willing to ride the wave, it can also be **one hell of a ride.**

The Players: Not All Cryptos Are Created Equal

Not all cryptos are made the same. In fact, there's a whole **hierarchy** in the crypto world, and knowing who's who can save you from making some rookie mistakes. Here's a quick rundown of the major players:

1. Bitcoin (BTC)

As I said before, **Bitcoin is the OG.** It's the first cryptocurrency, and it's still the biggest by market cap. Think of it as **digital gold**—a store of value that people turn to when they want to hedge against traditional markets. It's not the fastest or the most advanced coin out there, but it's got the **brand recognition** and the trust of the masses.

2. Ethereum (ETH)

If Bitcoin is gold, then **Ethereum** is like the **oil** that powers a whole new digital economy. Created by a kid genius named **Vitalik Buterin**, Ethereum introduced the concept of **smart contracts**—self-executing contracts with the terms written directly into code. This opened the floodgates for all kinds of decentralized apps (dApps), NFTs, and more. It's fast, it's innovative, and it's constantly evolving.

3. Altcoins

Any cryptocurrency that isn't Bitcoin is called an **altcoin**, and there are literally thousands of them. Some, like **Litecoin**, **Cardano**, and **Polkadot**, have strong communities and solid use cases. Others, like **Dogecoin**, started as a joke but somehow gained a massive following thanks to the internet and a few tweets from **Elon Musk**.

The trick with altcoins is that many of them are high-risk, high-reward. Some will soar to the moon, while others will crash and burn. So, do your research before putting your money in one of these.

The Hype Machine: What's the Deal with NFTs?

You've probably heard of **NFTs** (Non-Fungible Tokens) by now. If not, where have you been hiding? It seems like every other day, there's news of some random digital artwork or pixelated cat selling for **millions of dollars** as an NFT. So, what's the deal?

In simple terms, an NFT is like owning a **digital collectible**. It's a way to prove ownership of something unique in the digital world. It could be art, music, virtual real estate, or even a tweet. Unlike Bitcoin, which is fungible (meaning every Bitcoin is the same as any other Bitcoin), **NFTs are one-of-a-kind**.

Now, whether NFTs are here to stay or just another internet fad is still up for debate. But for now, they're a **hot commodity**, with artists, athletes, and influencers all jumping on the bandwagon.

Crypto and Regulation: The Elephant in the Room

Let's talk about the **giant elephant in the room**: regulation. As it stands, the crypto world is kind of like the **Wild West**—largely unregulated, chaotic, and full of opportunity for those who can handle the heat. But that might not last forever.

Governments around the world are starting to take a harder look at cryptocurrencies, and not all of them are thrilled with what they see. Some countries, like **China**, have already banned crypto mining and trading, while others, like the **U.S.**, are still figuring out their next move.

So, what does this mean for you as an investor? It's a bit of a double-edged sword. On one hand, **regulation could bring stability** and make crypto safer for the average person. On the other hand, it could also stifle innovation and limit the wild growth we've seen in recent years.

To HODL or Not to HODL: That Is the Question

Ah, the classic crypto dilemma: **Should you HODL?** For the uninitiated, "HODL" stands for **Hold On for Dear Life**, and it's become the battle cry of crypto investors who believe in **buying and holding** through the ups and downs, no matter how wild the ride gets.

But HODLing isn't for everyone. If you're someone who can't stomach seeing your investment drop 50% in a day (which can happen in crypto), you might want to reconsider your approach.

The Case for HODLing: Patience Pays Off

So, why do so many crypto enthusiasts swear by **HODLing**? Well, it's all about **long-term gains**. Sure, crypto is volatile—no one's denying that. But if you zoom out and look at the bigger picture, many of the folks who made it big in crypto did so by holding onto their investments even when the market tanked. They resisted the temptation to sell when prices dropped, knowing that the value could (and often did) bounce back.

Take **Bitcoin**, for example. Since its creation, Bitcoin has experienced some dramatic crashes. Yet, over the long run, it's continued to rise in value. Those who held onto their Bitcoin during the tough times ended up being rewarded handsomely when the price rebounded. It's like riding out a storm—you just have to be brave enough to stay on the ship.

Of course, **HODLing** isn't foolproof. There's always the chance that a particular cryptocurrency could fail entirely. But for those who believe in the long-term potential of crypto, **holding through the highs and lows** can be a smart strategy.

Timing the Market: Is It Even Possible?

Now, let's address the elephant in the room for anyone who isn't into the HODL life: **timing the market**. This is the holy grail of investing, right? Buy low, sell high, and laugh all the way to the bank. Sounds easy enough, but here's the thing—**it's incredibly hard to do**. In fact, most experts would argue that it's pretty much impossible to time the crypto market consistently.

Crypto prices can swing **wildly** in a matter of hours, sometimes even minutes. One minute you're celebrating a 20% gain, and the next, you're staring at a 30% loss. It's a rollercoaster, and unless you've got nerves of steel (or a crystal ball), it's tough to make the right calls every time.

That's not to say you can't make money by buying and selling crypto strategically. Some people do—those folks are usually called **day traders**, and they spend a ton of time analyzing charts, trends, and news to try to predict the next big move. But it's **not for everyone**, and it's definitely not a guaranteed way to make bank.

Crypto Scams: The Dark Side of the Wild West

Unfortunately, in a world as unregulated as crypto, there are always going to be **scammers** lurking around every corner. And boy, do they get creative. From fake ICOs (Initial Coin Offerings) to Ponzi schemes, phishing attacks, and rug pulls, the crypto world has seen its fair share of scams.

One of the most infamous scams in recent history was the **Bitconnect** debacle. Bitconnect was a cryptocurrency lending platform that promised investors massive returns on their Bitcoin holdings. For a while, it seemed to work—early investors saw big gains, and the hype kept building. But then, in January 2018, the whole thing came crashing down, with investors losing **billions**. It turned out Bitconnect was just a **classic Ponzi scheme**, paying old investors with money from new ones.

Moral of the story? **Do your research**. Don't just throw your money at any new coin that pops up with flashy promises. Stick to well-established coins or projects with a solid foundation and a **strong community**. And if something sounds too good to be true? It probably is.

Crypto Communities: It's More Than Just an Investment

One of the coolest things about the world of crypto is the **community**. It's not just about making money—well, okay, for some people it is—but there's a whole culture that's grown up around these digital currencies. Whether you're into **Bitcoin**, **Ethereum**, or any of the countless altcoins out there, chances are there's a dedicated community of fellow enthusiasts ready to chat, meme, and HODL right alongside you.

Online forums like **Reddit, Twitter**, and even **Discord** are buzzing with crypto talk 24/7. You'll find discussions on everything from the latest news to technical analysis, and of course, plenty of memes. The **"laser eyes" trend** on Twitter? Yeah, that's a thing where people literally put laser beams in their profile pictures to show their unwavering support for Bitcoin.

The point is, **crypto is more than just an asset class**. It's a movement. It's about decentralization, financial freedom, and pushing the boundaries of what's possible. And when you buy into crypto, you're not just buying an investment—you're joining a global revolution (or at least, that's how the die-hard enthusiasts see it).

Regulation Is Coming: Are You Ready?

Remember when I said the crypto world is like the Wild West? Well, the sheriff is coming to town. Governments and regulators around the world have started taking a much closer look at cryptocurrencies, and they're not exactly thrilled with what they see. **Tax evasion, money laundering, and fraud** are just a few of the issues they're concerned about.

In the U.S., the **SEC** (Securities and Exchange Commission) has been cracking down on certain aspects of the crypto space. For example, they've gone after several ICOs (Initial Coin Offerings) that they deemed to be unregistered securities. Meanwhile, countries like **China** have taken even more drastic measures, outright banning crypto mining and trading within their borders.

So, what does all this mean for you as an investor? Well, regulation could actually be a good thing in the long run. It might bring **stability** to the market and help protect investors from scams and bad actors. But in the short term, it could cause some volatility as governments figure out how to handle this new asset class.

Is Crypto Here to Stay?

Let's wrap things up by tackling the big question: **Is crypto the future, or just a passing fad?**

There's no denying that cryptocurrency has already had a massive impact on the world of finance. It's changed the way people think about money, investing, and even the internet itself (hello, **Web3**). But will it last? That's a trickier question.

Some people believe that **Bitcoin** and other cryptos are on their way to becoming **mainstream assets**—like gold or stocks. They see a future where crypto is used for everything from buying a cup of coffee to securing real estate contracts. Others are more skeptical, seeing the wild price swings, regulatory uncertainty, and rampant scams as signs that crypto's heyday could be short-lived.

One thing's for sure: **Crypto isn't going away anytime soon.** Whether it becomes the future of finance or just another speculative bubble that bursts, it's clear that digital currencies have captured the world's attention—and they're not letting go.

Final Thoughts: Should You Dive Into Crypto?

So, where does that leave you, the curious investor? Should you dive headfirst into the world of Bitcoin, Ethereum, and NFTs, or stick to more traditional investments like stocks and bonds?

At the end of the day, it all comes down to **your risk tolerance**. If you're the type of person who can handle the wild ups and downs, crypto could be a **fun and potentially rewarding** addition to your portfolio. But if the thought of losing 50% of your investment overnight makes you break out in a cold sweat, you might want to think twice.

Crypto is the **Wild West** of investing, and like any frontier, it's full of opportunity, danger, and excitement. If you're ready for the ride, **strap in**. Just don't forget to hold on tight.

INVESTMENT STRATEGIES THAT'LL MAKE YOU FEEL LIKE A PRO

Passive Investing: Set It and Forget It

So, you've probably heard the saying, "Time in the market beats timing the market," right? Well, that's basically the mantra of **passive investing**. Unlike those frantic day traders glued to their screens, passive investors are more like the chill surfers riding the slow, steady waves of the market. You're in it for the long haul, baby, and you're not sweating the day-to-day ups and downs.

Passive investing is about **simplicity, patience, and trust** in the long-term growth of the market. It's for the person who doesn't have time (or let's be real, doesn't want to make time) to track every tick of the stock market but still wants to see their money grow. Think of it as the "lazy genius" approach to wealth building. No stress, no constant checking, just set your strategy in place and let the market do its thing.

The Appeal of Passive Investing

Okay, let's get into why passive investing is like the ultimate easy button. First of all, **it's simple**. You don't need to be an investing wizard to pull this off. You just put your money into **low-cost index funds or ETFs** that track the market, and boom—you're an investor. Instead of trying to outsmart the market (spoiler: most people can't), you're just riding the overall market wave. And guess what? Historically, the market tends to go up over time. So, you're betting on the long-term success of the economy itself.

One of the biggest benefits of passive investing is that it saves you from the **rollercoaster of emotions** that comes with actively managing a portfolio. There's no need to panic when the market dips, and no temptation to sell when you get a sudden high. You're not chasing quick wins or trying to outguess the pros. Instead, you're building a **solid, slow-burning wealth** that compounds over time.

Another plus? **Low fees**. Actively managed funds often come with higher management fees, which can eat into your returns. Passive investments, on the other hand, typically have much lower fees because there's no superstar manager picking stocks. The beauty of an index fund is that it's tracking an entire market—whether it's the S&P 500 or a specific sector—and that means less fiddling around and fewer fees.

The "Set It and Forget It" Mentality

Here's where the "set it and forget it" comes into play. Once you've decided to go the passive route, you set up a plan, allocate your money to some well-diversified index funds, and let time work its magic. Sure, you'll want to check in every now and then to **rebalance** your portfolio (which we'll get into later), but for the most part, you're not obsessively refreshing your stock tracker app.

The whole point is to **stay calm and let the market do its thing**. There will be crashes, dips, and corrections—that's just how it goes. But history has shown that over time, the market tends to recover and grow. So, while some people are out there freaking out about short-term losses, you're sitting back, sipping your coffee, and watching your wealth grow like a slow-cooking pot roast. It's all about playing the long game.

How to Get Started with Passive Investing

So, you're sold on the idea of passive investing. Awesome! But how do you actually get started? Well, step one is understanding the **tools of the trade: index funds** and **ETFs**.

1. **Index Funds**: These are mutual funds designed to mimic the performance of a particular market index, like the S&P 500. Instead of handpicking individual stocks, an index fund spreads your investment across all the companies in that index. You get instant diversification, which means your risk is spread out too.

2. **ETFs (Exchange-Traded Funds)**: Similar to index funds, but they trade on the stock market like a regular stock. That means you can buy and sell them during market hours, and they often come with lower expense ratios (read: fewer fees). ETFs are great for people who like the idea of passive investing but want a little more flexibility in terms of trading.

Now, picking an index fund or ETF is the easy part—just look for low-cost options that cover a broad market. For example, if you want to invest in the U.S. stock market, something like the **Vanguard S&P 500 ETF** (VOO) is a solid choice. If you're looking for international exposure, you could consider the **iShares MSCI Emerging Markets ETF**. The key is to keep it simple. You don't need a hundred different funds to be diversified.

Once you've picked your fund(s), it's time to decide how much money to invest and how often. A lot of passive investors use the **dollar-cost averaging** strategy. This means you invest a fixed amount of money at regular intervals, whether the market is up or down. It's a smart way to avoid trying to time the market, and it smooths out your buying prices over time.

The Magic of Compounding

If there's one concept that passive investors love to geek out about, it's **compounding**. You've probably heard about it in high school math class, but let's be honest—you were probably more focused on passing notes. Here's the thing: **compounding is the secret sauce to long-term wealth**.

When you invest, you earn returns. But here's where it gets good: those returns start earning returns of their own. And those returns on your returns? They start growing too. It's like a financial snowball that just keeps getting bigger and bigger as it rolls down the hill.

Let's put it in perspective. Say you invest $10,000 in an index fund that averages a 7% annual return. After one year, you've got $10,700. But in year two, you're not just earning 7% on the original $10,000—you're also earning on that extra $700. Fast forward a couple of decades, and that $10,000 could turn into a small fortune without you lifting a finger. **That's the power of passive investing**.

Handling Market Volatility Like a Pro

We all know the stock market isn't a straight shot to the moon. There will be times when it feels like your portfolio is doing a free-fall into oblivion. But here's the thing about passive investing: **you don't panic**. You're not in this game to get rich overnight, and you know that market volatility is just part of the ride.

When the market drops, active investors are scrambling to figure out whether to sell, buy, or cry. But passive investors? They're more like, "Eh, I'll check back in a year or two." The whole point is that you're **riding out the rough patches** because you believe in the long-term growth of the market.

Now, that doesn't mean you should ignore your portfolio completely. It's important to keep an eye on your **asset allocation** to make sure it still aligns with your goals. Over time, certain parts of your portfolio might outperform others, which can throw off your balance. That's where **rebalancing** comes in.

Rebalancing: Keeping Your Portfolio on Track

Rebalancing is basically your way of checking in and making sure your portfolio doesn't get too out of whack. Let's say you've got a nice mix of stocks and bonds in your portfolio—maybe 70% stocks and 30% bonds. Over time, if the stock market does really well, your portfolio might end up being 80% stocks and 20% bonds, which might not be in line with your risk tolerance.

To rebalance, you'll want to sell some of the assets that have grown more than you'd like and buy more of the ones that have lagged behind. This keeps you aligned with your original plan and helps manage risk.

Most people rebalance once or twice a year, but there's no need to do it all the time. The beauty of passive investing is that you're not constantly tweaking your portfolio. You're just giving it a little nudge here and there to keep things on track.

The Long Game: Patience, Grasshopper

If there's one thing you need to succeed with passive investing, it's **patience**. This isn't about getting rich quick—it's about **getting rich slowly**. It's about understanding that the market will have ups and downs, but over the long run, it's going to grow. You just need to stick with it.

And let's be real: passive investing can be kind of boring. There's no daily drama of watching your stocks soar or crash. You're not glued to financial news or chasing the latest hot tip. But you know what? **Boring can be beautiful**. Because at the end of the day, it's not about excitement—it's about **building wealth** in a smart, sustainable way.

If you can handle a little boredom and trust the process, passive investing can be one of the most **rewarding financial decisions** you'll ever make. Just set it, forget it, and let your money grow.

Final Thoughts: Is Passive Investing Right for You?

So, is passive investing the right move for you? If you're someone who wants to build wealth over time without the stress of daily market fluctuations, then **absolutely**. It's a **low-maintenance, high-reward strategy** that has helped countless people achieve their financial goals.

Sure, it might not have the same adrenaline rush as active trading, but the peace of mind it offers is priceless. You're trusting the long-term growth of the market, and history has shown that this trust is usually well-placed.

Active Investing: Hustling in the Market

Alright, let's dive into the fast lane. **Active investing** is for those who love the thrill of the chase—the ones who are hustling, day in and day out, trying to beat the market. If passive investing is the laid-back surfer dude catching steady waves, active investing is the competitive speedboat racer cutting through the water, pushing for the win. It's about research, intuition, strategy, and—let's face it—a little bit of guts.

The goal here isn't just to ride the market wave—it's to **outperform it**. Active investors are the ones who believe that, with the right amount of know-how and the right moves, they can turn a better profit than your standard S&P 500 index. But it comes at a cost—more time, more energy, more risk, and definitely more drama.

What is Active Investing, Really?

Active investing is exactly what it sounds like: actively managing your investments. You're not just setting up your portfolio and forgetting it. Oh no, you're **in the trenches**, making decisions about which stocks to buy, when to sell, and how to rebalance your portfolio on the fly. You're studying financial reports, tracking company performance, listening to earnings calls, and probably checking the market on your phone while you're at dinner. (Guilty as charged.)

You're also looking at **trends**, doing technical analysis, and sometimes following the buzz around companies to spot opportunities. You might be eyeing **individual stocks**, trying to find that undervalued gem that everyone else missed. Or, you could be **day trading**, buying and selling assets within the same day to take advantage of price swings. It's high stakes and high intensity—definitely not for the faint of heart.

Active Investing: Hustling in the Market

The Allure of Beating the Market

So why do people choose active investing when the stats show that **most people underperform the market** over time? It's simple: the promise of **bigger gains**. When you actively invest, the idea is that you have a chance to beat the broader market and score higher returns than you'd get from passive investing. And yes, some folks actually do it.

There's something undeniably **sexy** about being able to say, "Yeah, I picked that stock before it blew up." It's the dream scenario—you buy shares of a little-known tech company at $10, and a couple of years later, you're sitting on a 10x return because it's now trading at $100. Cue the champagne, right?

But for every massive win, there are also some serious losses. Active investing is **risky business**. You could be riding high on a big gain one day, only to see it wiped out by a poor earnings report or some bad market news the next. The highs are high, but the lows? They can hurt. Active investors need to be able to stomach the ups and downs and stay cool under pressure.

The Tools of the Trade: Picking Stocks, Bonds, and Beyond

If you're an active investor, you've got a lot of tools at your disposal. The most common one? **Individual stocks**. When you're picking stocks, you're buying a piece of ownership in a specific company. Your goal is to pick stocks that you believe are going to increase in value over time.

But picking stocks isn't as easy as it sounds. You've got to dig deep into **financial reports**—we're talking income statements, balance sheets, and cash flow statements. You're looking for growth potential, a solid business model, competitive advantages, and sometimes even just a good story. You want to find companies that are undervalued by the market, meaning you're buying them for less than they're worth.

And let's not forget **bonds**. Active investors also play in the bond market, although it's usually less sexy than stocks. Bonds are like loans that you, the investor, give to a company or government. In return, they promise to pay you back with interest. While bonds are generally less risky than stocks, the risk comes from things like **interest rate changes** or the chance that the borrower (like a company) could default.

You might also be dipping your toes into more complex stuff like **options**, **futures**, or **commodities**. Options are contracts that give you the right (but not the obligation) to buy or sell a stock at a certain price. Futures work similarly but are tied to things like gold, oil, or even agricultural products. These are high-stakes moves—definitely not for beginners.

The Art of Timing the Market

One of the most famous sayings in investing is, "**It's not about timing the market; it's about time in the market.**" And while that might be true for passive investors, active investors are out here *trying* to time the market.

Timing the market means buying and selling based on your predictions about where the market is heading. Maybe you think the stock market is going to take a dive because inflation is out of control. Or maybe you believe a certain stock is about to skyrocket after the company announces a new product. Active investors make moves based on these predictions, trying to maximize gains and minimize losses.

But here's the kicker: timing the market is **incredibly hard**. Even professional investors with years of experience and access to loads of data often struggle to get it right consistently. Markets are unpredictable, and there are always outside factors—politics, natural disasters, global pandemics—that can throw your plans into a tailspin.

The key to active investing isn't just about having the right information—it's about knowing how to **interpret** it and having the guts to act on it. And sometimes, you're just gonna have to go with your gut.

Diversification for Active Investors: Don't Put All Your Eggs in One Basket

Even the most hardcore active investors know that **diversification** is crucial. Putting all your money into a single stock, no matter how much you believe in it, is a recipe for disaster. Sure, if it pans out, you could strike it rich. But if it flops? Well, there goes your entire portfolio.

Diversification means spreading your investments across different types of assets, like stocks, bonds, real estate, and maybe even some international markets. That way, if one of your picks goes south, it won't tank your whole game.

For active investors, though, diversification looks a little different than it does for passive folks. You might still be focused on individual stocks, but you'll want to make sure you're picking across different sectors—tech, healthcare, finance, etc.—to hedge your bets. You could also add some **international stocks** to get exposure to global markets.

And while active investors aren't typically as reliant on **index funds** as their passive counterparts, you might still want to sprinkle in a few ETFs to give you some broad-market coverage without having to pick every stock individually.

The Emotional Rollercoaster of Active Investing

If there's one thing that's constant in active investing, it's the **emotional rollercoaster**. One day, your portfolio is up 10%, and you're feeling like a genius. The next day, it's down 5%, and you're questioning every decision you've ever made.

Active investing can be emotionally draining. The **highs are exhilarating**, but the **lows can be devastating**. One of the biggest challenges for active investors is keeping their emotions in check. It's easy to get caught up in the excitement of a big win or to panic when things aren't going your way.

The best active investors know how to stay calm under pressure. They don't make impulsive decisions based on fear or greed. They stick to their strategy and trust their process, even when the market seems to be going haywire. That doesn't mean they're emotionless robots—it just means they've learned how to manage the emotional swings that come with the territory.

How to Get Started with Active Investing

Ready to start hustling in the market? First things first—you're gonna need a brokerage account. There are tons of options out there, from **Robinhood** to **E*TRADE** to **Charles Schwab**. Pick one that fits your style, whether that's commission-free trades or access to advanced research tools.

Once you've got your account set up, it's time to start building your portfolio. You'll want to decide on your strategy: are you looking to invest in **individual stocks**? Are you playing the **options market**? Or are you diving into something more niche, like **cryptocurrency** or **real estate investment trusts (REITs)**?

The most important thing is to **do your homework**. You can't just pick stocks based on a gut feeling (well, sometimes you can, but that's risky business). You need to research the companies, understand their financials, and stay on top of market trends.

And remember—active investing is all about staying on your toes. You'll need to monitor your portfolio, adjust your strategy as needed, and be ready to pivot when the market changes. **It's a full-time hustle**, but for those who thrive on the thrill, it can be incredibly rewarding.

The Risks of Active Investing: Know What You're Getting Into

Before you dive headfirst into active investing, let's talk about the **risks**. We've already mentioned that most people who try to beat the market **don't**. And if you're not careful, active investing can lead to some pretty painful losses.

First, there's the risk of **overtrading**. When you're constantly buying and selling, you're not just racking up potential gains—you're also accumulating transaction fees, taxes, and other costs. These can eat into your profits, making it harder to outperform the market in the long run.

Then, there's the risk of **emotional investing**. It's easy to get caught up in the hype when a stock is skyrocketing, or to panic-sell when it's plummeting. But making investment decisions based on emotions instead of logic is a surefire way to hurt your portfolio.

Finally, there's the risk of **time commitment**. Active investing is no joke—it takes a lot of time, effort, and dedication. You'll need to stay up-to-date on market news, company earnings, economic trends, and more. If you're not willing to put in the work, active investing might not be the best fit.

Final Thoughts: Is Active Investing Right for You?

Active investing isn't for everyone. It takes **time, knowledge, and a willingness to take on risk**. But for those who love the thrill of the chase and have the discipline to manage their emotions, it can be a rewarding way to build wealth.

If you're looking for a more hands-on approach to investing and believe you've got what it takes to beat the market, active investing might be the perfect fit. Just remember—it's a hustle, and like any hustle, there are no guarantees.

So, are you ready to **hustle**?

Long-Term vs. Short-Term: Playing the Field

When it comes to investing, everyone's playing the same game, but the **strategies**? Well, that's where things get interesting. In one corner, you've got the **long-term investors**—the cool, collected ones who swear by patience, compound growth, and the power of time. They're sipping iced tea on the porch, watching their investments grow slowly but surely, like a tree you planted years ago that's finally starting to bear fruit.

In the other corner, there's the **short-term crowd**—the adrenaline junkies who live for the thrill of quick gains. They're glued to their screens, riding the highs and lows of the market like it's a rollercoaster. These folks are making moves, hustling for those fast bucks. It's not about the long game; it's about what's happening **right now**.

But which one's right for you? The **tortoise** or the **hare**? The slow and steady path to financial freedom, or the quick and wild ride through the peaks and valleys of market madness?

Well, let's break it down, because the truth is, both approaches have their pros and cons. It's like dating, really—are you looking for a long-term relationship, or are you just playing the field, enjoying the excitement of the moment?

What's the Deal with Long-Term Investing?

Let's start with **long-term investing**. This is for the folks who believe in the magic of **compounding**—the idea that your money makes money, and then that money makes more money, and so on, like a snowball rolling down a hill, getting bigger as it goes.

The basic premise is simple: you **buy and hold**. You pick solid investments, like stocks, bonds, or mutual funds, and you hang on to them for the long haul—10, 20, 30 years, or even longer. The goal isn't to time the market or make quick trades, but to let the market do its thing over time.

Now, why does this work? Because historically, the stock market has a pretty reliable upward trajectory over the long term. Sure, there are crashes and corrections along the way, but if you zoom out and look at the big picture, the market tends to recover and grow. That's the beauty of long-term investing—you're not sweating the day-to-day swings. You're in it for the **big picture gains**.

Patience Pays: The Power of Time

One of the biggest benefits of long-term investing is that it takes advantage of the market's natural upward trend. Even if your investments hit a rough patch, time is your friend. Over the years, your portfolio has the chance to recover and grow, and that's where the magic happens.

Let's say you invest in the stock market at age 30. You put your money into a diversified portfolio of stocks and bonds, and you don't touch it for the next 30 years. During that time, the market will have its ups and downs—some years will be great, others will be rough. But over three decades, the overall trend will likely be upward.

The reason this works is because of **compound interest**. When you invest, your returns generate more returns, and those returns generate even more returns. It's like a snowball effect. The longer you leave your money in the market, the more time it has to grow, and the bigger your snowball gets.

The Emotional Rollercoaster (and How to Avoid It)

One of the most attractive parts of long-term investing is that you don't have to deal with the emotional rollercoaster that comes with day trading or short-term moves. You're not glued to your computer screen, obsessively checking stock prices every 10 minutes. You're not freaking out when the market drops 5% in a day because you know you've got decades ahead for it to recover.

In fact, long-term investors are often encouraged to **ignore** the short-term noise. The stock market is volatile—it moves up and down in the short term based on news, economic data, and investor sentiment. But over the long term, it tends to smooth out and grow.

So, if you're the kind of person who doesn't want to be **emotionally** tied to the market's daily drama, long-term investing might be for you. It's a more relaxed approach— set it, forget it, and let time do the heavy lifting.

Short-Term Investing: The Fast Lane

Now, let's talk about **short-term investing**. This is where things get a little more exciting (and a lot more nerve-wracking). Short-term investors aren't here to wait decades for their portfolio to grow—they're looking to **make moves** and pocket profits as quickly as possible.

For short-term investors, the focus is on **timing the market**. You're buying and selling stocks, bonds, or other assets within a short time frame—sometimes just days or weeks. The goal is to capitalize on price fluctuations, making money on the difference between what you paid for the asset and what you sell it for.

Sound stressful? That's because it is. Short-term investing is not for the faint of heart. You've got to be **on top of your game**, paying close attention to the market and staying ahead of the curve. You're tracking trends, reading financial news, and reacting quickly to changes. It's a lot of work, and it's definitely not as "set it and forget it" as long-term investing.

Playing the Field: The Risks and Rewards of Short-Term Investing

The biggest **draw** of short-term investing is that it offers the potential for **big gains** in a short amount of time. If you time your trades just right, you could see massive returns in days, weeks, or months.

But here's the catch: the potential for **big losses** is just as real. Short-term investors are riding the market's ups and downs, and if you make the wrong call, you could lose a lot of money fast. That's why it's so important to have a solid strategy and not just rely on gut feelings.

Short-term investing can be incredibly **lucrative**, but it's also a high-risk game. You need to be prepared for losses and be able to **handle the emotional swings** that come with it. If you're the kind of person who can't sleep at night because your stock portfolio is down 10%, short-term investing might not be for you.

Strategy: Long-Term vs. Short-Term

So how do you decide whether to go for a **long-term** or **short-term** strategy? It really comes down to your personal **risk tolerance**, your financial goals, and your temperament.

- If you're the kind of person who's okay with **delayed gratification** and can handle the ups and downs of the market without freaking out, long-term investing is probably your best bet. It's lower risk, less stressful, and generally leads to solid returns over time.

Long-Term vs. Short-Term: Playing the Field

- If you're someone who thrives on **excitement**, loves watching the market closely, and isn't afraid to take risks, short-term investing could be your jam. Just be prepared for the emotional highs and lows that come with it—and the potential for **big losses**.

Some people actually do both. They have a core portfolio of long-term investments (maybe an index fund or two), but they also set aside a smaller portion of their portfolio for **short-term trades**. This is sometimes called the "**core and satellite**" approach. The core is your safe, long-term money, and the satellite is where you take risks and try to score some short-term gains.

The Taxman Cometh: Tax Implications of Long-Term vs. Short-Term

One thing to consider when deciding between long-term and short-term investing is the **tax implications**. Uncle Sam loves to get his cut, and depending on how long you hold an investment, the amount you owe in taxes can vary significantly.

For **long-term investments**, meaning you hold the asset for more than a year, you'll pay **long-term capital gains tax**. The good news is that this tax rate is generally lower than what you'd pay on short-term gains. It ranges from 0% to 20%, depending on your income level.

For **short-term investments**, meaning you hold the asset for less than a year, you'll pay **short-term capital gains tax**. This is taxed as ordinary income, which means it could be as high as 37%, depending on your income bracket.

So, while short-term investing might offer the potential for quick gains, it also comes with a bigger tax bill. Long-term investors, on the other hand, benefit from lower tax rates, which can make a big difference over time.

Long-Term vs. Short-Term: Playing the Field

Diversification: The Key to Both Approaches

Whether you're a long-term investor, a short-term trader, or a little bit of both, one thing remains true: **diversification** is key. You don't want to put all your eggs in one basket, no matter what your investment timeline is.

For long-term investors, diversification means spreading your investments across a variety of asset classes—stocks, bonds, real estate, etc.—and across different industries and geographic regions. This helps to reduce risk and smooth out the bumps in the road.

For short-term traders, diversification might mean having a mix of different stocks, bonds, or even commodities in your portfolio. While you might be making quick trades, you still want to make sure you're not putting too much of your money into one risky bet.

Final Thoughts: What's Your Game Plan?

At the end of the day, the decision between **long-term** and **short-term** investing really comes down to your personal preferences, goals, and tolerance for risk.

If you're looking to grow your wealth over time, avoid the emotional rollercoaster of the market, and benefit from **compound growth**, long-term investing might be your best bet. It's the **slow and steady** approach that wins the race.

But if you're the type of person who loves the thrill of quick gains, enjoys tracking the market closely, and is willing to take on some **extra risk**, short-term investing could be the way to go. It's fast-paced, exciting, and potentially lucrative—but it's not without its challenges.

Long-Term vs. Short-Term: Playing the Field

Whichever path you choose, just remember: investing isn't a **one-size-fits-all** game. The most important thing is to find a strategy that works for you and stick with it. Whether you're in it for the long haul or playing the short-term game, stay focused, stay informed, and most importantly—**stay in the game**.

Value Investing: The Warren Buffett Way

Alright, let's talk **value investing**, folks. If investing was a superhero universe, Warren Buffett would be **Iron Man**—not because he's flashy, but because he's methodical, genius-level smart, and has this unshakable knack for making things work in the long run. Buffett's not about quick wins or chasing trends—he's about **value**. Cold, hard, undeniable **value**.

Now, if you're thinking, "Value investing, huh? Sounds boring," well, let me stop you right there. You might not get the same adrenaline rush as day traders, but you'll be riding a different kind of high—the sweet satisfaction of long-term, rock-solid wealth. Buffett's method isn't about **quick cash**; it's about stacking the deck in your favor and waiting for the right time to rake in the chips. You don't need a fancy suit or insider knowledge—all you need is patience, a sharp eye, and the willingness to play the long game.

The Basics: What the Heck is Value Investing?

Let's break it down in the simplest way possible. **Value investing** is basically the art of buying stuff on sale, but not just any stuff—**good stuff**. You're looking for stocks (pieces of companies) that are **underpriced**. These companies might be going through a rough patch, or maybe the market's just not paying attention. Either way, you swoop in, grab them at a discount, and hold on for dear life as they bounce back.

Think about it like this: you're walking into a high-end store, and you spot a designer jacket marked down 75%. Now, this jacket is still top quality, still made from the finest materials, but for some reason, nobody's paying attention. So, what do you do? You buy it, obviously. A few months later, that same jacket is back to full price, and everyone's wishing they'd snagged it when you did. That's **value investing**.

Warren Buffett's secret sauce is finding companies that are temporarily **out of favor** but have strong fundamentals. We're talking about businesses with great management, a durable competitive advantage, and solid financials—things that tell you, "Hey, this company is going to be around for the next 50 years."

Buffett's Mantra: Price vs. Value

Buffett's famous for saying, "**Price is what you pay, value is what you get.**" That's the essence of value investing. Just because something is cheap doesn't mean it's a bargain, and just because something is expensive doesn't mean it's overpriced.

Take Apple, for example. Back in the early 2000s, Apple stock was relatively cheap. People weren't exactly tripping over themselves to buy it. But those who recognized the company's **potential**—its innovation, its brand loyalty—saw that it was worth way more than its price tag suggested. Fast forward a few years, and Apple is the most valuable company on the planet. The lesson? **Look for value, not just a low price.**

The Search for the Golden Goose: How to Find Value

Finding undervalued stocks is like hunting for **gold nuggets** in a river of rocks. Most of the time, what looks like gold is just shiny pebbles, but every now and then, you strike it rich.

Here's where you start:

1. **Look at the Numbers**: This is where Buffett's analytical brain comes in. You're not just glancing at the stock

price—you're diving into the financials like a detective. Look at things like the **price-to-earnings (P/E) ratio**, the company's earnings history, debt levels, and whether they have a solid profit margin. The goal is to find companies that are financially sound but are being **undervalued** by the market.

2. **Understand the Business**: Buffett famously only invests in businesses he **understands**. This is a crucial step. If you don't know how a company makes money or how it plans to grow, why would you invest in it? Buffett sticks to industries he's familiar with—consumer goods, finance, utilities, etc. The lesson here is to **invest in what you know**.

3. **Durable Competitive Advantage**: Buffett looks for companies with a **moat**—something that protects them from competition. This could be a strong brand (think Coca-Cola or Disney), a unique product (like Apple's ecosystem), or even just being the low-cost leader in an industry (think Walmart). A company with a wide moat is less likely to get **overtaken** by competitors and more likely to deliver consistent returns over the years.

The Patience Game: Why Buffett Doesn't Day Trade

Warren Buffett isn't interested in buying stocks and flipping them for a quick profit. He's the master of **buy and hold**—the idea that you invest in a company and hold on for as long as it continues to create value. His favorite holding period? **Forever**.

Buffett's philosophy is rooted in **patience**. He's not swayed by the market's short-term swings or the latest investment fads. In fact, he often ignores the **daily noise** of the stock market altogether. When the market is down, he doesn't panic—he buys more. When the market is up, he doesn't sell in a frenzy—he holds tight.

And why? Because he knows that over the long haul, the **market rewards patience**. Companies with solid fundamentals tend to grow in value over time, and that's where the big money is made. It's not about timing the market—it's about **time in the market**.

Case Study: Coca-Cola—A Buffett Classic

Let's talk about **Coca-Cola**, one of Warren Buffett's favorite investments. Back in the 1980s, Coca-Cola was already a huge brand, but its stock was **underappreciated** by the market. People didn't quite see the potential for global domination that Buffett did.

Buffett recognized Coca-Cola's brand power, its distribution network, and its ability to sell sugary drinks to billions of people around the world. He saw that Coca-Cola had a **moat**—a wide one. It wasn't just selling soda; it was selling a lifestyle, a habit, and a brand that people were fiercely loyal to.

So, what did Buffett do? He loaded up on Coca-Cola stock, buying millions of shares. Fast forward to today, and Coca-Cola has paid him **dividends** for decades, and the stock price has soared. It's a classic example of value investing—finding a company that was **undervalued** at the time but had the potential to grow over the long term.

The Downside: It Ain't Always Glamorous

Let's be real—**value investing** isn't always glamorous. You're not going to get the same rush as someone making a quick buck off the latest hot tech stock or crypto token. And sometimes, you might have to wait **years** before your investments pay off. That's the downside.

You also need to have a **thick skin**. The market doesn't always behave rationally. Sometimes, the stocks you think are undervalued will stay undervalued for a long time, or worse, drop even lower. But Buffett's advice? Stay calm, stay patient, and don't let your emotions drive your decisions.

Value investing requires discipline, a long-term mindset, and the ability to **block out the noise**. It's not for everyone, but for those who stick with it, the rewards can be substantial.

The Buffett Checklist: Are You a Value Investor?

Want to invest like Warren Buffett? Here's a quick checklist to see if you've got what it takes:

- **You're patient**: You understand that the best returns often take years, even decades, to materialize.

- **You do your homework**: You're not just buying stocks because they're "cheap"—you're looking at the fundamentals and making informed decisions.

- **You're calm under pressure**: When the market tanks, you don't panic and sell. Instead, you see it as an opportunity to buy more.

- **You focus on quality**: You're not chasing trends or the latest hot stock. You're looking for companies with a strong competitive advantage, solid management, and the potential for long-term growth.

- **You're willing to go against the crowd**: Value investors often buy when others are selling. It takes guts to go against the grain, but that's where the bargains are.

Final Thoughts: The Buffet Legacy

At the end of the day, value investing is all about **finding diamonds in the rough**—companies that are temporarily undervalued but have the potential for long-term growth. Warren Buffett's approach has made him one of the richest people in the world, but it's not a get-rich-quick scheme. It's a strategy built on patience, discipline, and a keen understanding of what makes a business valuable.

If you're ready to dive into the world of value investing, remember the golden rule: **Price is what you pay, value is what you get**. Focus on the value, ignore the short-term noise, and let time work its magic.

Growth Investing: Riding the Rocket

Growth investing, my friends, is like strapping yourself to a rocket and hoping you land on the moon. It's about chasing the **big wins**—finding companies that are about to explode (in a good way) and taking off with them. Sure, there's some risk involved, but for those who are in it to **win big**, this strategy can take you to the next level.

We're not talking about playing it safe here—nope. If value investing is like planting a tree and watching it grow, **growth investing** is more like betting on the next Elon Musk. You're putting your money into high-growth companies that have the potential to disrupt entire industries, and yeah, that's as thrilling as it sounds.

What is Growth Investing, Exactly?

Here's the deal: Growth investing is about finding companies that are growing **faster** than the average. These are businesses that are reinvesting their profits into themselves to fuel expansion. You won't usually get dividends from growth stocks because they're too busy pumping money back into their operations, but that's okay because the value of your shares will (hopefully) skyrocket.

Think about companies like **Amazon** or **Tesla**. A decade or two ago, these were seen as risky investments. But those who spotted the potential early? Well, they're sitting on stacks of cash right now, laughing all the way to the bank.

Growth stocks typically trade at **higher prices** compared to their earnings (this is called a high P/E ratio), and that's because the market expects them to **keep growing**. Investors are willing to pay more today because they believe these companies will be worth much, much more in the future.

The Thrill of the Chase: Why Growth Stocks Are So Tempting

Okay, so why do people go crazy for growth stocks? It's simple: **the upside is huge**. While value investors are happy with a steady 5-10% annual return, growth investors are looking for returns of 20%, 50%, or even more. They're chasing the next **big thing**—the companies that will change the world.

And let's face it—there's something exciting about getting in on the ground floor of a company that's about to take off. You feel like you're part of the future, like you're not just investing in a stock, but in a **movement**.

But, let's not sugarcoat it—there's also a lot of **risk** involved. Growth stocks are more volatile than your blue-chip, stable value stocks. The price can swing wildly in a short amount of time. One day you're up 30%, the next day you're down 15%. You have to have the stomach for it.

How to Spot a Rocket Ship: Finding Growth Stocks

So, how do you spot the next **rocket ship** before it blasts off? You've got to do your homework. Growth stocks don't come with neon signs that say, "Hey, invest here for huge gains!" You've got to dig into the **fundamentals** and see what's really going on under the hood. Here are some key things to look for:

1. **Revenue Growth**: The first thing you want to see is a company's top-line growth. Are they making more money year over year? And I don't mean a little—growth companies are usually increasing their revenues by **double digits**. If a company is growing at 15%, 20%, or even higher, that's a good sign they're onto something big.

2. **Earnings Growth**: This one is a no-brainer. You want to see their **profits** increasing at a fast clip. It's one thing for a company to be growing its revenue, but if they're not turning that into profit, you might want to reconsider.

3. **Big Ideas**: Growth companies often have some kind of **disruptive technology** or business model that's shaking things up. They're not just following the crowd—they're leading it. Think about companies like **Netflix** when they changed the way we consume entertainment, or **Apple** with the iPhone. These weren't small innovations; they were **game-changers**.

4. **Management Team**: A growth company's management is super important. You want to make sure the people running the show have a vision and the ability to execute on it. Visionaries like **Elon Musk** or **Jeff Bezos** didn't just have cool ideas—they made them happen. Look for companies with **leadership** that's passionate and forward-thinking.

5. **Market Potential**: Is the company in an industry that's set to explode? Growth companies often operate in markets that are either new or rapidly expanding. Whether it's **tech**, **renewable energy**, **biotech**, or some other booming sector, you want to invest in a company that's in the right place at the right time.

The Roller Coaster Ride: The Risks of Growth Investing

If you're going to ride the rocket, you better be ready for some **turbulence**. Growth stocks are volatile—there's no sugarcoating it. You could be riding high one month, and the next month, you're watching your portfolio take a nosedive. Why? Because growth companies are usually reinvesting everything into expansion, which makes them more sensitive to market conditions.

Here are some risks to keep in mind:

1. **High Valuations**: Growth stocks often trade at sky-high prices relative to their earnings. This is because investors expect future growth to justify the high price. But if that growth doesn't materialize as expected? Well, the stock could take a big hit. It's like paying for a fancy sports car and finding out it has a faulty engine.

2. **Competition**: Growth companies are often operating in fast-moving, innovative sectors where competition is fierce. A hot new startup could quickly take market share from a growth stock you've invested in, and that could spell trouble for your returns.

3. **Regulatory Risk**: Growth companies in industries like **tech** or **biotech** often face regulatory challenges. Governments can step in and throw a wrench in the works, especially if a company is getting too big for its britches. We've seen this with **Facebook** and **Google** in recent years.

4. **Market Sentiment**: Growth stocks are heavily influenced by market sentiment. If investors lose confidence, the price can plummet quickly, even if the company is doing well. You've got to be ready for these wild swings and not panic-sell when things go south.

Case Study: Tesla—The Ultimate Growth Rocket

No discussion of growth investing would be complete without talking about **Tesla**. Love him or hate him, Elon Musk has turned Tesla into one of the most **explosive** growth stocks in recent history.

Back in the early 2010s, Tesla was seen as a **risky bet**. The company wasn't profitable, it was burning cash, and people weren't sure if electric cars would ever catch on. But those who believed in Musk's vision? They've been rewarded beyond their wildest dreams.

Tesla's stock went from trading in the **double digits** to over **$1,000** per share in a matter of years. Why? Because the company wasn't just selling cars—it was revolutionizing an entire industry. Tesla tapped into the global push for **clean energy**, created cars that people **wanted**, and built a brand that was synonymous with **innovation**.

But here's the kicker—along the way, Tesla's stock price was a roller coaster. It had **huge dips**, and at times, people thought the company might go under. That's the nature of growth investing. Those who stuck with it are now laughing, but it wasn't an easy ride.

The Patience of a Growth Investor: It's Not Always Fast

Despite the name, growth investing requires **patience**. Sure, the goal is to find stocks that will grow at an explosive rate, but that doesn't mean they'll grow quickly overnight. It might take years for a company to hit its stride and for the market to fully recognize its potential.

You've got to be willing to wait out the **bumps**. Just like Warren Buffett advises with value investing, growth investors need to take a **long-term view**. You're betting on the future, and that takes time.

The Growth Investor's Checklist

Before you jump into the world of growth investing, here's a quick checklist to make sure you're ready for the ride:

- **You're comfortable with risk**: Growth investing is not for the faint of heart. You have to be okay with volatility and the potential for losses in the short term.

- **You believe in the future**: Growth investors are optimists. You're betting that the companies you invest in will change the world—or at least their industry.

- **You're willing to do the research**: Finding growth stocks isn't easy. You need to dive into the numbers, understand the business, and follow industry trends closely.

- **You're patient**: Even though growth stocks have the potential to grow rapidly, it doesn't always happen overnight. You've got to be in it for the long haul.

- **You can handle the highs and lows**: Growth stocks are volatile. One day you're up 50%, the next you're down 20%. If you can't handle the swings, growth investing might not be for you.

Final Thoughts: Ready for Liftoff?

Growth investing is exciting. It's about identifying the next **big thing**, the companies that will shape the future and drive massive returns for those who get in early. It's not a smooth ride, and there are plenty of risks along the way, but for those who are willing to strap in and ride the rocket, the rewards can be astronomical.

So, are you ready to take your investing to the next level? Buckle up, because this rocket is about to launch.

MANAGING RISK LIKE A BOSS

Diversification: Don't Put All Your Eggs in One Basket

Picture this: You're walking through a busy street market, and you're carrying this **big ol' basket** filled with eggs. Fresh, pristine eggs. Now, we all know that if you drop that basket, you're not just losing one egg—**you're losing everything**. Not a great situation, right? That's exactly what happens when you fail to diversify your investments. You're betting everything on one outcome, one asset, one stock. And if it goes south, well... you're left scrambling (pun intended).

What is Diversification, Anyway?

Diversification is a fancy word for **spreading your risk**. It's about not putting all your money into one single investment because if that investment crashes and burns, so do your finances. Instead, by spreading your investments across different **assets**, **sectors**, and even **geographies**, you can reduce your risk. In simpler terms: if one investment tanks, you've got others that might balance things out.

Here's how it works in the most basic sense: Imagine you're buying stocks. Instead of investing all your money in just **one company**, you invest in 10 different companies from various industries. If one company hits a rough patch, the others might still do well, softening the blow.

It's like building a **team of superheroes** instead of relying on just one to save the day. Sure, Superman is awesome, but what if he's busy with kryptonite? That's when you need Batman, Wonder Woman, and the rest of the gang to step in.

Why Diversification Matters: A Reality Check

Let's talk straight: the world is unpredictable. Markets fluctuate. The economy goes up and down. One year tech stocks are killing it, and the next year, energy stocks might be soaring while tech is in the dumps. If you're betting everything on one sector or one stock, you're at the mercy of that **one piece of the puzzle**.

Take **Enron**, for example. In the late '90s, it was one of the most admired companies in America. People trusted it, invested in it, and believed it would keep growing forever. But when Enron collapsed in 2001, people who had all their money in that stock **lost everything**. Had they diversified, their portfolios might've been saved by other investments that weren't caught up in the scandal.

This isn't just true for stocks, either. Think about **real estate** or **cryptocurrency**. These are volatile markets that can have **huge** swings. If you've got all your money tied up in just one type of asset, you're setting yourself up for either a big win or a big loss. Diversification is about **playing it smart**.

Building a Diversified Portfolio: The Recipe for Success

Now, let's get to the meat of the matter—how do you actually build a diversified portfolio? It's like cooking a meal: you want to include a variety of ingredients to make sure you've got a well-rounded dish. Same goes for investing. You want a mix of different types of investments so that you're not relying on just one.

Here are the **key ingredients**:

1. **Stocks**: This is the main course for most investors. But even within stocks, you want to spread it out. Invest in different **sectors**—like tech, healthcare, consumer goods, and energy. Don't just buy Apple, Tesla, and Netflix. Look at more traditional industries, too.

Diversification: Don't Put All Your Eggs in One Basket

2. **Bonds**: Bonds are like the steady, reliable side dish. They won't give you massive returns, but they'll provide stability. When the stock market goes wild, bonds tend to keep things on an even keel. It's like having mashed potatoes with your steak—it's dependable.

3. **Real Estate**: Real estate is another key player in a diversified portfolio. Whether you're investing directly in properties or through **REITs** (Real Estate Investment Trusts), having some exposure to real estate can provide a hedge against the ups and downs of the stock market.

4. **Commodities**: These are things like **gold**, **oil**, or **agricultural products**. Commodities often perform well when stocks are struggling, so they can add another layer of protection.

5. **Cryptocurrency**: Now, I'm not saying you should put a ton of money into crypto, but a small portion of your portfolio in assets like **Bitcoin** or **Ethereum** could give you exposure to an emerging market with a potentially massive upside. But remember, crypto is **super volatile**—it's like adding hot sauce to your dish. A little goes a long way.

6. **International Investments**: Don't just stick with US companies. Look at international markets, too. Europe, Asia, emerging markets—they all offer different growth opportunities. Sometimes the US market is down while the **global market** is booming. It's like sampling different cuisines from around the world.

The Benefits of Diversification: Smooth Sailing in Rough Waters

So, what do you get when you diversify? You get **peace of mind**, that's what. Diversification helps you **smooth out the ride**. Instead of wild swings where your portfolio is up 20% one day and down 15% the next, you're more likely to have steady growth. Sure, you won't get the crazy highs, but you also won't suffer the devastating lows. It's about **minimizing risk** while still chasing returns.

Imagine being on a ship in the middle of the ocean. If a storm comes, wouldn't you rather be on a big **cruise ship** than a little rowboat? Diversification is that big cruise ship—it helps you weather the storms without capsizing.

And here's the thing—diversification isn't just about risk reduction. It also increases your chances of **catching a winner**. When you're invested in a variety of assets, one of them could take off and deliver those **big returns**. But if you're not diversified, you might miss that opportunity altogether.

The Common Mistakes: How Not to Diversify

Now, just because diversification is important doesn't mean you can do it **haphazardly**. Here are some common mistakes people make when trying to diversify:

1. **Over-diversification**: Yes, there's such a thing as too much diversification. If you're investing in 50 different stocks, you might be spreading yourself too thin. You want **quality over quantity**. Focus on making strategic choices rather than just throwing money at everything.

2. **Ignoring Correlation**: Just because you have investments in different areas doesn't mean you're truly diversified. Some assets are highly **correlated**, meaning they move in the same direction. If you're investing in tech stocks and growth stocks, even if

they're in different industries, they might still tank at the same time.

3. **Not Rebalancing**: A lot of investors diversify at first, but then they don't adjust their portfolios over time. If one of your investments has grown significantly, it might now represent too large a portion of your portfolio. You need to **rebalance** regularly to keep things in check.

4. **Forgetting International Exposure**: A lot of US investors stick with US companies. But by doing that, you're missing out on global opportunities. Remember, markets around the world move differently. Diversifying internationally is crucial.

Case Study: The 2008 Financial Crisis

Let's take a trip down memory lane to the **2008 financial crisis**. It was a nightmare for investors, but those who had diversified portfolios fared much better than those who were all-in on real estate or financial stocks.

People who had put all their money into real estate-related investments, like **mortgage-backed securities** or bank stocks, got hit hard. But those who had a mix of stocks, bonds, and international assets saw less of a dramatic decline. The stock market was down, yes, but **bonds held steady**, and international markets started to recover faster.

Diversification didn't prevent losses entirely—nothing can do that—but it **softened the blow**. Instead of being wiped out, diversified investors were able to weather the storm and recover more quickly.

How to Diversify with ETFs and Mutual Funds

Diversification: Don't Put All Your Eggs in One Basket

If the idea of picking individual stocks, bonds, and real estate sounds overwhelming, don't worry—there's an easier way. You can diversify by investing in **ETFs** (Exchange Traded Funds) or **mutual funds**. These are basically baskets of different assets that you can buy with one click.

For example, an **S&P 500 ETF** will give you exposure to the 500 largest companies in the US. That's instant diversification. Or, you could invest in an **international ETF** to get exposure to global markets. There are even **sector ETFs** if you want to focus on areas like tech, healthcare, or energy without putting all your eggs in one company.

Mutual funds work in a similar way, though they're actively managed, which means a fund manager is picking the stocks for you. Both are great options for diversifying without the headache of choosing individual investments.

Diversifying Over Time: The Power of Dollar-Cost Averaging

One of the best ways to diversify is by using a strategy called **dollar-cost averaging**. Instead of dumping all your money into the market at once, you invest a fixed amount regularly—say, every month or every quarter. This means you're buying more shares when prices are low and fewer when prices are high, which helps smooth out your returns over time.

Let's say you have $12,000 to invest. Instead of putting it all in at once, you could invest $1,000 a month. This way, if the market drops, you're not taking the hit all at once. And if prices go up, you're still buying in over time. It's like adding a pinch of salt to your meal as you cook rather than dumping the whole container in at once.

The Bottom Line: Diversify Like a Pro

At the end of the day, **diversification** isn't some magical formula that guarantees success, but it's one of the smartest strategies you can use as an investor. By spreading your money across different assets, sectors, and geographies, you're giving yourself the best shot at building a strong, resilient portfolio that can handle whatever the world throws your way.

Investing isn't about making quick cash—it's about building **long-term wealth**. And if you want to keep your eggs safe, make sure you've got more than one basket. It's as simple as that.

Rebalancing: Keep Your Portfolio in Check

Alright, let's get real: **rebalancing** is like a reality check for your portfolio. Picture your portfolio as a garden—you plant all these little seeds (your investments) with care, expecting them to grow in harmony. But here's the catch: some plants shoot up like they're on steroids, and others... not so much. Before you know it, that neat little garden is a jungle. **Rebalancing** is how you tame the wild growth, keeping everything in balance so your investments stay on track.

What is Rebalancing, Anyway?

At its core, rebalancing means adjusting your portfolio to get back to your original plan. Let's say you decided that **60% of your money** should go into stocks, **30% into bonds**, and **10% into real estate**. Over time, those allocations drift as markets move. Maybe now stocks are taking up **75%** because they had a great year, while bonds shrank to **15%**. Rebalancing means selling a little bit of that runaway growth in stocks and redistributing it back into bonds and real estate.

Think of it as **giving your portfolio a regular tune-up**. It's like taking your car in to make sure all the parts are working as they should be. You're not just "setting it and forgetting it"—you're checking in, making sure everything's aligned, and giving it a nudge here and there.

Why Bother with Rebalancing?

Good question. Why can't you just let your winners run, right? The answer is all about **risk control**.

1. **Keeping Risk Levels in Check**: Imagine you set up your portfolio with a certain amount of risk in mind.

Let's say you're okay with 60% in stocks because, historically, they're a bit more volatile. But if your stocks are now at **80%** of your portfolio, suddenly you're way more exposed to the ups and downs of the stock market than you originally planned. Rebalancing brings you back to your comfort zone.

2. **Taking Profits from the Highs**: Rebalancing forces you to sell some of your investments that have **performed well**. This might feel counterintuitive—why sell a winner? But by selling when they're high, you're locking in those gains and using them to boost your laggards, the underdogs that haven't yet had their time to shine.

3. **Avoiding Emotional Decision-Making**: When you have a clear rebalancing strategy, you're less likely to make rash decisions based on market swings. You're not panicking because the market's down or making a mad dash to buy more when it's up. You're simply **following a plan**.

The How-To Guide for Rebalancing

So, how often should you rebalance? Some folks do it annually, others quarterly, and some even **rebalance based on percentage drift**. Let's break down the main methods.

1. Calendar-Based Rebalancing

This one's simple: You choose a set time to rebalance, like at the end of each year, quarter, or month. It's like giving your portfolio a birthday check-up. You're setting a routine, which keeps things straightforward and easy to remember. But remember, markets can change quickly, so sticking strictly to dates without looking at market movements might mean you miss some big shifts.

2. Percentage-Based Rebalancing

In this approach, you rebalance when an asset class (like stocks or bonds) drifts a certain percentage from your original allocation. Let's say you're okay with a 5% drift. If your 60% stocks grow to 65% or fall to 55%, that's your trigger. This method can be more dynamic since it responds directly to market movement. It's like adjusting the thermostat when the room gets too hot or too cold—it keeps your portfolio closer to your target.

3. Rebalancing with New Investments

If you're adding new money to your portfolio regularly, you can use those fresh funds to rebalance without selling anything. Say stocks are up, and bonds are down. Instead of selling stocks, you just buy more bonds with your new money. It's a slick, tax-efficient way to rebalance without realizing any capital gains.

Common Rebalancing Mistakes

Let's talk about some pitfalls to avoid when you're rebalancing.

1. **Rebalancing Too Often**: It can be tempting to rebalance every time the market shifts, but overdoing it can lead to excessive trading fees and taxes. Plus, you might lose out on long-term gains by jumping in and out too frequently.

2. **Ignoring Transaction Costs**: Every time you rebalance, there are potential transaction fees and taxes. Make sure you're aware of these costs before you start selling and buying like there's no tomorrow.

3. **Rebalancing During Market Panics**: When the market's in a tailspin, it's easy to let emotions take over. But rebalancing out of fear can backfire. Stick to your plan, even if the market is making you nervous.

4. **Not Factoring in Taxes**: Selling investments to rebalance can trigger capital gains taxes, especially in taxable accounts. Try to rebalance in tax-advantaged accounts (like IRAs) when possible, or use new contributions to avoid triggering taxes.

The Benefits of Rebalancing in Action

Let's look at an example. Imagine you set up a portfolio in **2009**, right after the financial crisis. You go with 60% stocks, 30% bonds, and 10% real estate. Over the next decade, stocks have an incredible run, soaring way past your other investments.

By 2019, you're looking at a portfolio that's now 80% in stocks, 15% in bonds, and 5% in real estate. You're feeling great because your portfolio's worth way more, but it's also way more **risky** than it was when you started. By rebalancing, you'd be forced to **sell some of those stocks**, take profits, and reinvest in bonds and real estate. You're locking in those gains and ensuring you're not overexposed if stocks take a hit.

How Rebalancing Ties into a Long-Term Strategy

Rebalancing isn't about **timing the market** or chasing short-term gains. It's a disciplined approach that keeps you focused on your long-term goals. It's like keeping your ship on course. Even if you drift, regular rebalancing steers you back in the right direction, preventing you from straying too far off track.

Imagine you're hiking a trail with a map. As you walk, the terrain shifts, and you might veer a little off-path. Rebalancing is like checking that map every so often to make sure you're still heading toward your destination. It's not glamorous, but it works.

When Should You Rebalance?

Rebalancing doesn't have a one-size-fits-all answer. It depends on factors like your risk tolerance, goals, and investment strategy. But here are some general rules:

- **After Major Market Movements**: Big market shifts, like the 2020 pandemic crash, are often a good time to check in on your portfolio.
- **When Your Goals Change**: If you're nearing retirement, you might want to shift from growth-focused stocks to more stable bonds and cash.
- **At Least Once a Year**: A yearly check-up keeps you from drifting too far, even if you don't have strict percentage rules.

Rebalancing in Retirement: A Different Game

Once you're retired, rebalancing takes on a new role. Instead of focusing solely on growth, you're balancing risk while ensuring you have enough **income** to live on. Retirees often need to shift from a growth-heavy portfolio to a more **income-focused one**. It's all about preserving what you've built.

In retirement, rebalancing can mean **selling investments to fund your lifestyle** or rebalancing more conservatively to avoid big losses.

The Emotional Side of Rebalancing: Taming the Nerves

Let's face it: rebalancing can feel a bit like being forced to clean up a party when it's in full swing. Your winning investments are doing great, and here you are—being all responsible by taking a portion of those gains and spreading them around. It's human nature to want to ride the winners and ignore the underperformers. But remember: *the purpose of rebalancing is to keep your portfolio in harmony.*

The trick is to **stay cool** and **stick to your plan**, even when emotions run high. Market highs and lows can be nerve-wracking, but rebalancing forces you to be a little more zen about it all. It's a reality check, reminding you that you're in this for the long haul.

Real-Life Stories of Rebalancing Gone Right (and Wrong)

Story 1: The Disciplined Investor

Meet Sam. Sam's been investing since he was 25, and he sticks to a rebalancing schedule every year. In 2021, when tech stocks were on fire, Sam was tempted to let his tech-heavy portfolio ride the wave. But he followed his plan, selling off a bit of his tech stocks and putting that money into bonds and real estate. Fast forward to 2022, when the tech bubble burst—Sam was grateful he rebalanced. His portfolio was shielded from a significant drop, and he didn't lose as much as he would have if he'd gone all-in on tech.

Story 2: The All-In Gambler

Then there's Mike. Mike loves the thrill of the market and thinks rebalancing is for people who aren't brave enough to chase big returns. He invested everything in crypto and tech stocks, ignoring his original allocation. For a while,

Mike's portfolio was soaring, and he felt like a genius. But when both markets tanked, Mike's portfolio took a major hit. If he'd rebalanced, he would have locked in some profits and buffered against the loss.

Making Rebalancing Work for You

The beauty of rebalancing is that it's customizable. You can make it as frequent or infrequent as you like. Want to do it **quarterly**? Go for it. Prefer to check in every December? That's cool too. The key is to find what works for you and stick with it.

Here are some final tips to keep in mind:

1. **Automate When Possible**: Some brokerages offer automatic rebalancing tools, which can take the pressure off you and ensure you're staying disciplined.

2. **Consider Tax Implications**: Always think about taxes when rebalancing in taxable accounts. In retirement accounts, this isn't an issue, but in taxable accounts, you might want to avoid big capital gains bills.

3. **Stay True to Your Goals**: Rebalancing isn't about maximizing returns—it's about keeping risk in check and staying aligned with your financial goals. Keep your eyes on the big picture.

The Bottom Line on Rebalancing: The Secret to Staying Balanced

Rebalancing is like the unsung hero of investing. It doesn't get the spotlight like hot stock tips or market timing, but it quietly works behind the scenes, helping you keep your portfolio on the straight and narrow. It's a practical, level-headed approach that keeps you from getting carried away, and over the long haul, that steady discipline can make a world of difference.

So, whether you're a novice just dipping your toes in the investing waters or a seasoned pro with years of experience, rebalancing is your friend. It's the habit that keeps your garden of investments looking its best, no matter what the market throws your way. **Stay disciplined, stick to the plan, and let rebalancing do its magic.**

Investment Insurance: Protecting Your Wealth

Alright, let's talk about something that doesn't sound as exciting as "growth stocks" or "crypto," but it's something that can keep you afloat when the seas get rough—**investment insurance**. Now, I know what you're thinking: *Insurance? Sounds boring.* But here's the deal—investment insurance is like that unsung hero who shows up right when you need them. It might not make you rich overnight, but it sure can help you *stay* rich (or at least, *not get poor*).

Why Even Think About Investment Insurance?

Imagine you're on this journey, riding the highs of the market and watching your portfolio soar. Then, out of nowhere, a market crash hits. Stocks plummet, real estate tanks, and even the safest of assets take a beating. *But what if you had something in place to soften that fall?* That's what investment insurance is for. It's like a seatbelt for your portfolio—a little protection so you don't end up face-first in financial disaster.

Think of it this way: if you wouldn't drive a car without insurance, why would you put your hard-earned money out there without some protection? It's not glamorous, but *it's smart*.

Different Types of Investment Insurance

So, what are the options here? It turns out, there are a few ways to approach protecting your wealth, and they range from "oh, that makes sense" to "wait, you can insure that?" Here's a look at some key types:

1. **Standard Insurance Policies**
   These are your basic **life, health, and disability**

insurance policies. Think of them as the bread and butter of investment insurance. While they might not directly cover your stocks or bonds, they protect your income. Without income protection, a bad accident or illness could force you to liquidate investments early—never a good thing.

2. **Long-Term Care Insurance**
   This one's a biggie for those looking at retirement planning. Long-term care costs can be brutal. Having insurance for this means you won't need to drain your portfolio to cover these costs later on in life.

3. **Annuities**
   Annuities are kind of the "insurance-meets-investment" deal. You hand over a chunk of cash to an insurance company, and in return, you get a steady income for life (or however long the term is). It's a way to insure you'll have a paycheck no matter what's going on in the market. Just remember: not all annuities are created equal, so read the fine print.

4. **Portfolio Insurance**
   Now we're talking. This is insurance on *your actual investments*. Options, futures, and derivatives might sound like a foreign language, but they can actually be used to protect your portfolio. Let's say you've got a big chunk of your money in stocks. You can buy options to protect yourself from massive losses if the market tanks.

5. **Diversification as "Insurance"**
   You've probably heard that diversification is the one free lunch in investing. By spreading out your investments across various asset classes—stocks, bonds, real estate, maybe a little crypto—you're protecting yourself from any one asset class taking you down.

A Deep Dive into Annuities

Alright, let's go a little deeper into annuities, because they can be both *incredibly useful* and *maddeningly complex*. Essentially, an annuity is an agreement with an insurance company where you pay them either a lump sum or a series of payments, and in return, they agree to pay you a steady income.

There are a few flavors of annuities:

- **Fixed Annuities** – Think of these as the steady, boring option. You get a set payment every period, no matter what's happening in the market. *The stock market could be having the time of its life or going down in flames; your check stays the same.*

- **Variable Annuities** – With these, your income depends on the performance of the underlying investments. So, if the stock market's doing great, you'll get a bigger payout. If it's not? Well, your income could shrink. *High risk, high reward*, as they say.

- **Immediate vs. Deferred** – An immediate annuity starts paying you right away. A deferred annuity, on the other hand, starts paying at some future date. Deferred annuities are common in retirement planning because you can let that money grow (tax-deferred) before cashing in.

Are Annuities for Everyone?

Not exactly. *Annuities can be expensive*, and once you put money into an annuity, it's not always easy to get it out. They're also not particularly flexible. So, if you're young and still building your wealth, you might want to hold off. But for people approaching retirement who are looking for guaranteed income, they can be a lifesaver.

Investment Insurance: Protecting Your Wealth

Diversification as a Form of Insurance

Let's bring it back to something a little simpler: **diversification.** You've probably heard people say "don't put all your eggs in one basket." Well, diversification is like the grown-up version of that advice. The goal here is to have a mix of assets so that when one part of the market is down, something else in your portfolio is likely to be up (or at least steady).

Here's why it works: different types of investments tend to move in opposite directions. *Stocks and bonds*, for instance, often don't correlate. When stocks are down, bonds might be doing just fine. Real estate might be on fire, while tech stocks are cooling down. Having a bit of everything helps you avoid huge losses.

Real-Life Insurance Wins and Fails

Case 1: The Conservative Saver Consider Sarah, who was conservative by nature and opted for a healthy mix of insurance policies and investments. She had life, health, and long-term care insurance, plus a nice, diversified portfolio. When she was hit with some unexpected medical costs later in life, her insurance policies covered the bulk of it, allowing her to keep her investments intact. Her diversified portfolio also helped her weather the ups and downs without much stress.

Case 2: The Risk-Taker Then there's Jake. Jake went all-in on tech stocks, refusing to even look at insurance or alternative investments. He figured he was young, healthy, and had time on his side. When the tech bubble burst, he lost big—so big that he ended up having to delay his retirement and get a second job. Jake learned the hard way that having some insurance on his portfolio (either through options or diversification) could have saved him a lot of heartache.

Insurance on Your Investments: Options and Futures

Alright, so you're ready to go all-in on protecting your actual investments. Options and futures can seem intimidating, but they're essentially contracts that give you more control over your portfolio.

- **Options** – Think of options as a type of "mini-insurance." You pay a fee (called a premium) for the right, but not the obligation, to buy or sell a stock at a certain price. So if the market goes haywire, you're not left hanging.

- **Futures** – Futures are more like a legally binding agreement. You agree to buy or sell something at a set price in the future. They're riskier but can work as insurance if used wisely.

These aren't tools that every investor needs, but if you're dealing with a large or volatile portfolio, they can offer some solid protection.

The Psychology of Protection: Why It's Hard to Think About Insurance Until You Need It

Insurance, in general, isn't the most thrilling topic. A lot of people ignore it because it feels like *planning for the worst*, which isn't exactly the most uplifting mindset. But protecting your wealth doesn't have to be about expecting disaster; it's just a savvy move for anyone who wants to sleep a little better at night.

THE NITTY-GRITTY: GETTING STARTED WITH PRACTICAL TIPS

Opening a Brokerage Account: The First Step

So, you're ready to dip your toes into the world of investing. You've heard about stocks, bonds, maybe even crypto, and you're eager to get in on the action. But here's the kicker—you've got to have a brokerage account to get started. It's like the gateway to the investment world, and opening one is that *first, big step* towards building wealth. *Feels kinda exciting, right?*

But let's be real—there's a lot of noise out there about which brokerage to choose, what fees to consider, and all these fancy investment terms that can make the process feel like you're signing up for a new job. *Fear not*, because this guide is about to break it all down for you in simple, straightforward language. By the end, you'll be ready to open your account, dive into the market, and *start hustling*.

Why Do You Even Need a Brokerage Account?

Alright, first things first—why even bother? A brokerage account is like the toolbox that lets you build your financial future. You can't buy stocks, ETFs, mutual funds, or bonds without one. It's like trying to join a gym without a membership. And sure, you could go old-school and stick with a savings account, but you won't get that *potential for growth*. With a brokerage account, you're stepping into the game where your money can actually make you more money. It's the difference between letting your cash sit around doing nothing and giving it a job.

Different Types of Brokerage Accounts

Opening a Brokerage Account: The First Step

Let's clear this up right away: not all brokerage accounts are the same. You've got a few different flavors to choose from, depending on your goals. Here's the quick lowdown:

1. **Individual Taxable Accounts**
   This is the go-to option for most folks. It's straightforward, flexible, and lets you buy and sell whenever you want. However, Uncle Sam will want his cut, which means you'll pay taxes on dividends, interest, and capital gains. But hey, that's the price of freedom, right?

2. **Retirement Accounts (IRA, Roth IRA)**
   If you're looking to invest for the long haul (think retirement), then an IRA (Individual Retirement Account) is worth considering. There's a traditional IRA, where you get a tax break upfront, and a Roth IRA, where you get the tax break when you take the money out. *And yes, tax benefits are a big deal.* These accounts come with some rules about when you can withdraw, but they're great for long-term goals.

3. **Joint Accounts**
   If you're looking to invest with a partner—whether it's a spouse, sibling, or business partner—a joint account could be the way to go. Just remember, you're both on the hook, so choose wisely!

4. **Custodial Accounts**
   Got a little one you want to set up for future financial success? A custodial account is basically an investment account for minors. You manage it until they're old enough to take the reins.

Picking the Right Brokerage for You

With so many brokerage firms out there, it can feel like you're walking into an ice cream shop with *too many flavors*. Each one's got its own set of perks, fees, and platform features. Here's what to consider:

1. **Fees, Fees, Fees**
   Some brokerages charge you every time you buy or sell, while others are more like, *"Hey, trades are on the house!"* Look for low or no-commission options, especially if you're just starting out and plan to make small trades. You don't want to be losing money before you've even made any.

2. **User-Friendly Platforms**
   You're looking for an app or website that doesn't make you feel like you're hacking into NASA. Some platforms are super intuitive and great for beginners, while others are packed with tools that might be overwhelming for a newbie. Take a peek at some screenshots, maybe try out a demo if they offer one.

3. **Research Tools and Education**
   Some brokerages offer great research tools and educational resources, which are gold when you're learning the ropes. Look for one that offers access to market data, analysis, and tutorials to help you learn as you go.

4. **Customer Service**
   If something goes wrong, you want a brokerage with solid customer support. Whether it's chat, phone, or email, reliable customer service can be a lifesaver when you're dealing with your hard-earned cash.

The Step-By-Step Guide to Opening Your Account

Opening a Brokerage Account: The First Step

Alright, time to roll up those sleeves and get down to business. Here's what you need to know about actually *opening* the account.

1. **Gather Your Personal Info**
   Most brokerages are going to ask for the basics: your name, address, Social Security number, and probably your employment info. *Pro-tip: if you're not comfortable sharing certain details, check the brokerage's privacy policy.*

2. **Choose Your Account Type**
   We talked about this earlier, but it's time to decide. Are you going for a regular taxable account? A retirement account? Choose the one that fits your goals best, but remember, you can always open multiple types down the line.

3. **Fund Your Account**
   Here comes the part where you actually put some skin in the game. Most brokerages will let you link a bank account to transfer funds directly. You can start with as little or as much as you're comfortable with, depending on the brokerage's minimum requirement (some have none).

4. **Set Up Any Additional Features**
   Some brokerages offer nifty tools like automatic investment plans, dividend reinvestment options, and more. If you're new, you might want to keep things simple at first, but as you get comfortable, these features can be super handy.

What to Watch Out for as a New Investor

The investment world can be a bit of a jungle, especially for a newbie. Here are some things to keep on your radar as you jump in:

- **Don't Go All In Right Away**
  It's tempting to throw your money at the "next big thing," but investing is a marathon, not a sprint. Start small, get a feel for the market, and *learn as you go*. There's no rush.

- **Avoid High Fees**
  Fees can seriously eat into your gains. Look out for annual fees, transaction fees, and any sneaky hidden charges. Sometimes, a brokerage might look free on the surface but hide fees in fine print, so read carefully.

- **Stay Calm with Market Ups and Downs**
  When the market's riding high, you might feel like a genius. When it dips, it's easy to feel like pulling everything out. *Don't panic*. Market swings are part of the game, and learning to ride them out is key.

Common Questions People Have When Opening a Brokerage Account

Here are a few questions you might have bouncing around as you open up your account:

1. Can I lose money?
Short answer: yes. Long answer: any investment carries risk, but that's also where the reward comes from. The key is to invest in a way that fits your comfort level.

2. What if I don't know what to invest in?
Many brokerages offer "robo-advisors," which are basically algorithms that can help you choose investments based on your goals and risk tolerance. They're not perfect, but they're a solid start.

3. How much should I start with?
The amount depends on your goals and comfort level. Some people start with $50, others with $5,000. *It's more*

about consistency than starting with a fortune. Start small if you're nervous, then increase as you get comfortable.

Choosing a Broker: Who's Got Your Back?

Alright, so you've made it this far, and now we're getting to the part where the rubber really meets the road: **picking your broker**. Imagine your broker as your *financial BFF*—the one who'll help you build your future. Picking the right one can make or break your investing journey, so let's dig in and make sure you choose a broker who's truly *got your back*.

Why Choosing the Right Broker Matters

Alright, think about this: the stock market is like a giant playground with endless swings, slides, and jungle gyms of investments. But you can't just walk in and start playing. *You need a guide,* someone who'll let you into the playground and help you navigate it. That's where a broker comes in. A broker is basically your ticket into the world of stocks, bonds, ETFs, and a ton of other investment goodies.

But there's a catch. Not every broker is the same. In fact, they're all wildly different, with their own personalities, strengths, and quirks. Some might charge you every time you make a move; others could care less if you're a buy-and-hold type. And then there's customer service, platform usability, and all those little things that *make or break* your experience.

Types of Brokers: From Full-Service to DIY

Here's where things get real interesting. Brokers come in a few different flavors, and what you pick depends on *how much hand-holding* you want along the way. Let's break it down:

1. **Full-Service Brokers**
   Imagine having a personal financial guru who's there

to hold your hand, give you advice, and help you make the big calls. Full-service brokers are *the VIP treatment* of the brokerage world. They'll assign you an actual human advisor who'll help guide your choices. But... they don't come cheap. Full-service brokers charge hefty fees, so unless you're sitting on a nice pile of cash, this option might not be worth the splurge.

2. **Discount Brokers**
    Here's where most people end up. Discount brokers are like *middle-of-the-road* options: they give you access to the market without all the bells and whistles. You won't have a dedicated advisor, but you'll still get tools, research, and a platform to make your trades. Discount brokers tend to be budget-friendly and great for people who are ready to do some of their own digging. Think names like Fidelity, Charles Schwab, or TD Ameritrade.

3. **Robo-Advisors**
    Want someone—or something—to take the wheel entirely? Enter the robo-advisor. Robo-advisors use algorithms to manage your portfolio. They're perfect if you're looking for a hands-off approach. You just answer a few questions, and the robo-advisor will invest your money based on your goals and risk tolerance. It's like having a financial robot looking out for you. Just remember, while they're super affordable, you won't get that personal touch.

4. **Online Brokers**
    We're in the digital age, and online brokers are the cool, tech-savvy siblings of traditional brokers. Companies like Robinhood, E*TRADE, and Webull fall into this category. They're app-based, often commission-free, and make investing feel like a breeze. Just remember: online brokers can be super

convenient but might not have all the research tools or customer service of traditional brokers.

Questions to Ask When Choosing Your Broker

Okay, let's say you've got a shortlist. Here's where you really dig deep. Ask yourself these questions:

1. **What's their fee structure?**
   Fees can sneak up on you if you're not careful. Some brokers charge per trade, others have annual fees, and some—like robo-advisors—take a cut of your assets. Make sure you're not shelling out more than you need to.

2. **How user-friendly is the platform?**
   You don't want to feel like you're navigating a maze every time you log in. Check out their interface, read some reviews, or even test out a demo. Some platforms are built for pros, while others make it *easy for everyone*.

3. **What's the minimum deposit?**
   Some brokers require a minimum to open an account, while others don't. If you're starting small, make sure your broker doesn't require a ton of cash upfront.

4. **What resources do they offer?**
   Especially if you're new, having access to research tools, stock analysis, and tutorials can be a game-changer. Some brokers have extensive resources, while others are bare-bones.

5. **How's their customer service?**
   You hope you'll never need it, but if you do, having a broker with solid customer support is key. Imagine your account gets locked, and you can't reach anyone. *Not fun.*

Choosing a Broker: Who's Got Your Back?

Popular Brokers and What They're Known For

Now, let's get into some *big names* and why people love (or hate) them.

1. **Fidelity**
   Known for its strong research and customer service, Fidelity is a discount broker with a *wide range* of investment options and educational resources. Great for folks who want a trusted name with a solid track record.

2. **Robinhood**
   Ah, the disruptor. Robinhood's known for making investing accessible with its commission-free trades. However, it's been controversial for a few reasons, including outages and a bit of a *Wild West* vibe.

3. **Charles Schwab**
   Schwab's got something for everyone: low fees, solid customer support, and a great mix of research tools. They've also got branches nationwide, so you can actually go in and talk to someone if you need to.

4. **Betterment**
   If you're all about that robo-advisor life, Betterment's one of the best. With low fees and solid performance, they're ideal for people who want hands-off investing.

5. **E*TRADE**
   E*TRADE is a solid all-rounder, offering a nice mix of investment options, decent fees, and a user-friendly interface. They also have great customer service and are known for their educational resources, making it perfect for new investors who still want flexibility and access to more complex trading.

6. **Webull**
   Webull is another popular choice for folks who want a mobile-focused, commission-free broker. They offer great charting tools, which is appealing to active traders, but the platform is slightly more complex, so it's a better fit for those who have a bit more experience.

Fee Types: Know the Damage Upfront

Every broker has its unique way of charging fees, and knowing how these fees work can save you a lot of cash in the long run. Here's a quick rundown of what to look out for:

- **Trading Fees**: Some brokers charge every time you buy or sell a stock, ETF, or option. These fees can be flat (e.g., $5 per trade) or based on the size of your trade. Many online brokers, though, are moving to *zero commission* for certain types of trades.

- **Account Maintenance Fees**: Some brokers charge a monthly or yearly fee just to keep your account active. Not super common these days, but always worth double-checking.

- **Advisory Fees**: If you go with a robo-advisor or a managed account, they'll usually take a small percentage of your portfolio value as a management fee.

- **Withdrawal Fees**: Some brokers charge you for taking your own money out—wild, right? Make sure you know if they've got limits on how much and how often you can withdraw without a penalty.

- **Inactivity Fees**: If you open an account and then ghost your broker, some will charge you for not trading. If you're planning to be a buy-and-hold investor, look for brokers who don't penalize you for taking a break.

Safety and Security: Is Your Money Safe?

Alright, real talk—when you're trusting someone with your hard-earned cash, you want to know they're legit. Here are a few key safety features to look for:

1. **SIPC Insurance**: This is a biggie. The SIPC (Securities Investor Protection Corporation) protects your brokerage account for up to $500,000 if the firm goes bust. It doesn't cover you if your investments lose value (that's just the market doing its thing), but it's there to protect you from a broker going belly-up.

2. **Two-Factor Authentication (2FA)**: It's always nice to have that extra layer of security. Brokers with strong digital security measures, like 2FA, help keep your account safe from hackers.

3. **Reputation and History**: Established brokers with a long track record (think Fidelity, Schwab) tend to be safer bets. Newer brokers can still be great, but it's worth looking into their background and checking for any sketchy history or fines.

Setting Up Your Account: The First Steps

Once you've chosen a broker, setting up your account is usually a breeze. Here's a quick step-by-step on what to expect:

1. **Sign Up Online**: Most brokers let you open an account right from their website or app. You'll fill out a bunch of basic info, like your name, address, and

Social Security number (they're required by law to collect this).

2. **Choose Your Account Type**: You'll generally have a few options, like a standard brokerage account, a retirement account (like an IRA), or a custodial account if you're setting one up for a kid. Most people start with a standard brokerage account, but if you're saving for retirement, an IRA has some sweet tax benefits.

3. **Answer Risk Questions**: Brokers will usually ask about your income, investing experience, and risk tolerance. This helps them recommend investments that fit your style (although with discount brokers, it's just for info—they don't give personalized advice).

4. **Link Your Bank Account**: To fund your account, you'll need to link your bank account. Most brokers make this part super easy, so you can transfer money back and forth without fees.

5. **Start Investing!**: Once your account is funded, you're ready to hit the ground running. Whether you're buying stocks, ETFs, or mutual funds, this is where the fun starts.

The Endgame: Picking the Broker That Works for YOU

At the end of the day, there's no "one size fits all" broker. It's about finding the one that fits your style, your budget, and your goals. Maybe you want something hands-off and automated—*robo-advisor to the rescue*. Or maybe you're all about getting into the weeds with charting tools—hello, Webull.

So, take your time, explore your options, and *don't feel pressured*. Choosing a broker is a big decision, but once you've got the right one in your corner, you'll be set up to invest confidently, knowing you've got a solid partner in your financial journey.

Why Analyze Companies Like a Detective?

Ever wondered how Sherlock Holmes cracks his cases? He digs for clues, picks up on little details, and pieces everything together until he sees the big picture. Now, imagine that same approach applied to analyzing companies. This isn't about looking at a single snapshot, it's about seeing *the whole story*.

Think of it this way: every company out there, big or small, is hiding a treasure trove of clues. They're all wrapped up in financial statements, leadership structures, and industry trends—just waiting for you to crack the case. And why should you? Because the better you know a company, the better you'll know if it's worth investing in!

The Case of the Balance Sheet: Unmasking Assets, Liabilities, and Equity

A company's balance sheet is like a financial snapshot: it shows what the company owns and owes at any given time. This is *Clue #1*.

1. Assets: What's in Their Arsenal?

Assets are what a company *owns*. Picture them as the detective tools they have on hand—their resources to grow and get ahead. From cash reserves and real estate to intellectual property, assets tell you what a company has at its disposal to drive profits.

- **Current Assets**: Quick cash and stuff that's easy to sell—*like inventory*. It's Sherlock's magnifying glass and notebook: tools ready to be used.
- **Long-Term Assets**: Think buildings, patents, trademarks. These are the high-tech detective

gadgets Sherlock brings out for tough cases; they're stable, powerful assets that offer long-term value.

2. Liabilities: What Do They Owe?

Liabilities, on the other hand, are like the company's "IOUs." From short-term debts to long-term loans, it's what they owe to others. *A big pile of liabilities could signal trouble.* It's like our detective hero's cases piling up without any chance of resolution. But a manageable amount? That's just par for the course in the business world.

3. Equity: The Stake in the Game

Finally, we have *Equity*. This represents the owners' stake in the company after all liabilities are paid off. Equity is like the reward for solving the case, the treasure at the end of the mystery. Strong equity often signals that a company's in it for the long haul, with a stable foundation that could lead to profitable growth.

Income Statement: Following the Money Trail

If the balance sheet shows what a company has, the income statement shows how it's earning its keep. Here, you'll track the *revenue, expenses, and net income.* Let's dive into each:

1. Revenue: The Company's Main Attraction

Revenue is the cash coming in from what the company does best. Think of revenue as the "bounty" on the case. Sherlock wouldn't be chasing clues if there wasn't some kind of payoff, right? In the same way, a business that's consistently bringing in revenue is actively solving its own puzzle of growth.

2. Expenses: The Necessary Evils

Now, for a business to earn that revenue, it incurs expenses. We're talking about the costs of materials, wages, rent, and all that jazz. Keeping a close eye on expenses can reveal where a company might be *bleeding cash*. High expenses aren't always bad; sometimes, they mean the company is investing in its future. But runaway expenses with no return? That's like Sherlock losing focus—*big warning sign!*

3. Net Income: The Real Prize

After all expenses are paid, we're left with the *Net Income*, aka profit. Think of it as the grand "Aha!" moment when Sherlock solves the case. High, steady net income? That's a company that's doing well and making money consistently. Fluctuating income? It could mean the company's facing some big challenges, or maybe it's just in a highly competitive industry. Either way, *Net Income* gives you a sense of the company's real health.

Cash Flow Statement: Sherlock's Secret Weapon

Money coming in, money going out. That's what the *Cash Flow Statement* is all about. It's like the heartbeat of a business.

1. Operating Cash Flow: Day-to-Day Detective Work

This is the cash that comes from the company's main business activities. Strong, positive cash flow here means the company has enough dough to keep the lights on and run its day-to-day operations.

2. Investing Cash Flow: Future Cases

This section covers investments in assets or other companies. If a company is spending cash here, it might be buying equipment, investing in tech, or acquiring another business. These moves may not pay off immediately, but they're like

Sherlock gathering new skills or equipment—*investment in the future*.

3. Financing Cash Flow: Paying Debts and Issuing Stock

This part is all about how the company finances its operations—like issuing stock, paying dividends, or paying back debt. Positive financing cash flow isn't necessarily a good thing if it's coming from massive borrowing. Likewise, negative cash flow here isn't always bad if it means the company is paying off debt or buying back stock.

Ratios: Sherlock's Magnifying Glass

Ratios help you analyze the numbers in context, comparing companies or looking at a company's performance over time. Let's break down a few key ratios:

1. **P/E Ratio (Price-to-Earnings)**
   This is like checking how pricey a stock is compared to its earnings. High P/E? The market's got high hopes for future growth. Low P/E? Maybe there's some skepticism. Or it could be a hidden gem waiting to be discovered!

2. **Debt-to-Equity Ratio**
   How much debt is the company rocking compared to its equity? High debt-to-equity might mean higher risk, but it could also mean a growth strategy in play.

3. **Return on Equity (ROE)**
   ROE shows you how efficiently a company is using its equity to generate profits. A high ROE? That's usually a great sign of solid management and effective use of resources.

Putting the Puzzle Together: Analyzing Qualitative Clues

Why Analyze Companies Like a Detective?

Crunching the numbers is essential, but to really understand a company, we need to look at the *story behind the numbers*. Here's where you switch from just being Sherlock to being Sherlock *and* Watson—piecing together hard data with a gut feeling.

1. The Management Team: Who's Calling the Shots?

Behind every great company is a team of people making the big calls. Research the leadership team to get a sense of their background, experience, and track record. Are they seasoned pros with a history of turning companies around? Or are they newbies still figuring things out?

- **Consistency** in leadership often translates to consistency in results.
- **Visionary leadership** could mean a company with a bright future ahead.

2. Industry Trends: Is the Market Hot or Not?

A company may be killing it now, but if its industry is in decline, it's like riding a sinking ship. On the other hand, a rising industry could give even struggling companies a chance to thrive. It's key to *understand the bigger picture* and where the company sits in the industry cycle.

3. Competitive Position: Who's in the Lead?

Understanding a company's competitors is just as crucial as understanding the company itself. Are they the big fish in a small pond, or a small fish in a big ocean? Companies with a strong competitive advantage often fare better long-term because they're tougher to beat.

Red Flags and Green Lights: Spotting Good and Bad Signs Early

Why Analyze Companies Like a Detective?

As you analyze, keep an eye out for potential red flags that could spell trouble—and green lights that indicate smooth sailing ahead.

Red Flags ⚑

- **Consistently Negative Cash Flow**: If a company is regularly spending more than it's making, that's usually a bad sign.
- **High Debt Levels**: Debt isn't inherently bad, but if it's piling up without a solid plan for repayment, it could mean trouble.
- **Unstable Leadership**: Frequent changes in the C-suite can signal chaos behind the scenes.

Green Lights ✓

- **Steady Revenue Growth**: Shows a company that's doing something right and attracting customers.
- **Low Debt-to-Equity Ratio**: This often indicates a stable, well-managed company with controlled risk.
- **Innovative Edge**: Companies that are industry innovators tend to weather economic changes better than those who simply follow the trends.

Case Closed: Making the Call

Once you've gathered the clues, it's time to make the big decision. Is this company a go or a no? Here's where you pull all the evidence together.

- **If the numbers check out, the industry is thriving, and the management team is solid,** you could be looking at a winning investment.

Why Analyze Companies Like a Detective?

- **But if red flags are flying high, or the company's growth potential seems limited,** it may be best to pass and find another case to crack.

And there you have it—analyzing companies like a pro detective. Sherlock would be proud. Now, it's your turn to hit the market with this new sleuthing skill set. Trust your gut, read between the lines, and remember: even in investing, every clue counts.

Analyzing Companies: Sherlock Holmes Mode

Alright, rookie investor, welcome to the **detective side of investing**. This isn't just looking at spreadsheets and numbers—it's about seeing through the data, spotting clues, and figuring out whether a company is a diamond or a dud. When you're in Sherlock Holmes mode, every number, every strategy, every market move is a clue. *Elementary, my dear Watson*, right? Or maybe not, but by the end of this chapter, you'll have the skills to think like the ultimate investment detective.

The Investigation Begins: Knowing What to Look For

Imagine you're a detective, standing at the threshold of a mysterious case. You have your **company profile**—your basic suspect sheet—but now you need to dig deeper. You're looking at the *DNA of the business*, understanding what makes it tick, and figuring out if it's all it's cracked up to be. Here's the first stop:

1. Understand the Business Model: How Does It Make Money?

Think of the business model as a company's **recipe for success**. For instance, Starbucks makes money by selling coffee, but their model is much more layered than that. They're all about creating a community experience, tapping into trends like mobile ordering, and yes, strategically placing shops on every corner.

Ask yourself:

- **What exactly does this company do?** Are they selling products, services, or a combination?
- **How do they make their money?** Look at their main revenue streams—are they diversified or reliant on a single source?

- **What sets them apart?** If the company's model isn't unique, what's stopping others from copying it?

Companies that have strong, unique models and revenue streams are like suspects with rock-solid alibis. They're reliable, and that's a good start.

The Plot Thickens: Diving into Financial Statements

Alright, Watson, it's time to **put on the reading glasses** (or blue light glasses, because 21st-century detective work means screens). Financial statements are like the company's diary, but unlike teenage scribbles, these numbers don't lie. Here's where you go full Sherlock:

Income Statement: What's the Bottom Line?

This is where you see if the company's bringing in the dough. But don't just look at net income—look at **revenue**, **expenses**, and **operating income**.

- **Revenue** shows what they're making from sales. Is it growing steadily, or are there sudden drops?
- **Operating Income** gives you a look at how well they're managing costs versus what they're bringing in.
- **Net Income**: The final number. Are they in the red or black?

Pay special attention to **trends over time**. A strong income statement is the sign of a company that knows how to keep the money flowing, which is a big green flag.

Balance Sheet: A Snapshot of Stability

Think of this as a **company's financial selfie**. Here, you get a picture of their assets, liabilities, and equity. It answers the question: *If this company had to pay off all its debts tomorrow, could it?*

- **Assets**: What they own (cash, property, investments).
- **Liabilities**: What they owe (debts, loans, obligations).
- **Equity**: What's left after liabilities. This is the shareholders' slice of the pie.

In Sherlock terms, a company with **more assets than liabilities** is a good suspect—less likely to be hiding skeletons in the closet.

Cash Flow Statement: Is the Money Moving?

Cash flow is the **heartbeat** of any company. It shows if a business has enough money to keep going, pay its bills, and invest in the future. Pay close attention to **operating cash flow**—this tells you if the company is generating cash from its core business.

- **Positive cash flow** is like finding out your suspect pays their bills on time.
- **Negative cash flow**, especially if it's a pattern, might signal trouble ahead.

Company Culture and Management: Who's Running the Show?

Sometimes, it's not just about the *what*—it's about the **who**. A lot can be said about a company by understanding who's steering the ship and the culture they've created. Good management is like a reliable detective team—they work together, adapt to challenges, and keep the company on track.

- **Management's Background**: Do they have experience in the industry, or are they new kids on the block?
- **Employee Satisfaction**: Happy employees often mean a company that's being run well. Check out sites like Glassdoor to see if the vibe is positive or toxic.
- **Innovative Spirit**: Companies that embrace change and innovation tend to grow. Look for signs they're investing in R&D or entering new markets.

Understanding the Industry: Who Else Is Playing the Game?

A company isn't an island; it exists within a market, alongside competitors. Analyze the **competitive landscape** to see where it stands.

- **Is it a leader, follower, or challenger?**
- **Does it have any unique advantages** over competitors?
- **What's the market demand?** For example, a solar energy company might have a solid future due to growing demand for renewable energy.

A company with a strong position in a booming industry is like a detective who always has an inside scoop.

Looking for Red Flags and Green Lights

With every good detective story, there are clues that point towards both guilt and innocence. Here are some financial red flags (uh-oh!) and green lights (yes!) to look out for.

Red Flags: Signs of Trouble

- **Excessive Debt**: Companies drowning in debt often have a hard time investing in growth or weathering economic storms.
- **Declining Revenue**: If sales are dropping consistently, they're losing ground to competitors or facing industry challenges.
- **Frequent Leadership Changes**: Management turnover could mean instability.

Green Lights: Signs of Strength

- **Steady Revenue Growth**: Growing sales over time shows people like what the company's selling.
- **Low Debt**: Companies with low debt often have more flexibility and resilience.
- **Consistent Dividends**: If a company is paying dividends steadily, it's a sign of financial health.

Piecing it All Together: The Final Verdict

After all the analysis, it's time to make the big call. Is this a company worth betting on, or does something smell fishy? As Sherlock would say, "When you have eliminated the impossible, whatever remains, however improbable, must be the truth."

1. **If the business model is strong, the numbers add up, and management is on point**—it's a likely winner.
2. **But if the red flags are waving high**—it's probably best to pass.

The art of analyzing companies is like the thrill of solving a mystery. With practice, patience, and these tools in hand, you're ready to start cracking the case on your next investment decision.

Analyzing Companies: Sherlock Holmes Mode

Glossary of Terms:
Because let's face it, no one remembers all this jargon the first time around. Here's a cheat sheet for your inner Sherlock.

Exercises:
Ready to apply your detective skills? Check out these exercises to start sharpening your analysis on real-world companies.

CONCLUSION: YOU GOT THIS – KEEP GOING!
Wrapping It All Up

Alright, look at you! You made it through an entire book on investing. Give yourself a high-five, grab a cup of coffee (or something stronger if it's that kind of day), and get ready to *soak up the golden nuggets* we've uncovered. You've done the hard part of showing up, getting curious, and pushing through the nitty-gritty, and now, there's only one direction left to go: up!

What You've Learned So Far: Your Investment Cheat Sheet

If this book were a treasure map, we'd be at the X—marking everything essential that'll help you navigate the complex and wild world of investing. Let's break it down one more time, hitting the highlights:

1. The Mindset of an Investor: Ready, Set, Think Like a Pro

The first step in your journey was all about your *mindset*. You've got to think like a savvy investor, not just someone who throws cash at the latest trendy stock. Remember:

- *Investing is a marathon, not a sprint.* Quick returns can be tempting, but slow and steady often wins the race.
- You're in it for the *long haul*. Real growth comes over time, not overnight.
- Keep emotions in check. The stock market might be a rollercoaster, but your job is to stay steady and strategic.

2. Portfolio Power: Don't Put All Your Eggs in One Basket

Diversification isn't just a fancy term; it's your *best friend*. By spreading your investments across different asset types—

stocks, bonds, maybe even some real estate—you're giving yourself a cushion. Here's what to remember:

- *Spread the risk.* Different assets react differently to market changes, so having a balanced mix protects you.
- Diversify within asset classes too. Even if you love tech stocks, don't put every dollar into one sector.
- Regular rebalancing is key. The goal is to keep your portfolio working hard for you, without putting it at unnecessary risk.

All the Tools and Tricks: Building a Strategy

Now you know the basics of building a portfolio, but *tools make the craftsman*. Here's a refresher on the major moves and strategies we covered.

Analyzing Companies Like a Pro

Think Sherlock Holmes meets Wall Street. Analyzing a company is all about:

- **Understanding its business model**: How does it make money?
- **Financial health check**: Read those income statements, balance sheets, and cash flow statements like clues in a mystery novel.
- **Industry position**: Where does the company stand in the big, bad world of competition?

Remember, when you dig into a company's finances, you're doing the detective work to find out if it's worth your hard-earned cash.

Choosing the Right Broker

This part wasn't just about finding someone to handle your trades; it's about finding someone who's got your back. Choose a broker with:

- **Solid customer service**: Investing can be complicated, so a broker who can explain things simply is a gem.
- **Low fees**: Why pay more than you need to?
- **Great tools and resources**: A broker with an easy-to-use platform and educational resources is worth their weight in gold.

The Bigger Picture: Long-Term Wealth Building

Now, here's the *secret sauce*: Long-term wealth building is all about consistency. You don't have to be perfect; you just have to keep showing up. Here's the final checklist for keeping on track:

- **Stick to your goals**: Having a clear goal helps you stay focused and patient.
- **Keep learning**: Investing isn't a one-and-done kind of deal. Keep up with trends, read financial news, and adapt as markets change.
- **Reinvest dividends**: If you're investing in dividend stocks, reinvesting can compound your gains over time.
- **Review your portfolio regularly**: Stay on top of your investments to make sure they're still aligned with your goals.

Why This Isn't the End, Just the Beginning

Wrapping It All Up

You've read this far, and guess what? You're miles ahead of most people who never took the time to really understand their money. Now, the world of investing is your oyster. You've got the skills, the tools, and the confidence to keep growing your wealth, making smart choices, and building a future on *your* terms.

Investing is a journey, not a destination. You'll learn new things, make adjustments, and maybe even have some wild stories to tell along the way. But no matter what, you'll be one of the few who took charge of their financial future. So give yourself credit—this is big.

One Last Piece of Advice? Keep It Real.

There will be ups and downs, and no one has all the answers. But if you stick to what you've learned here, keep things real, and stay curious, there's nothing you can't achieve. Financial freedom is yours for the taking.

Motivation to Keep Crushing It

Alright, rockstar, you've made it here with grit, guts, and a killer focus on your future. This chapter? It's all about *keeping that fire* burning and pushing you to go even further. You've got the tools, you've built a solid foundation, and now? It's time to put the pedal to the metal. Investing, after all, isn't just a one-time thing. It's an *ongoing adventure*, a marathon that keeps rewarding you the longer you're in it.

You're on the Path – So Keep Walking!

Here's the truth: *Building wealth is a journey*, not a destination. It's not about "getting rich" as fast as possible. Nope. It's about creating something sustainable, something that'll take care of you and your loved ones for years to come. And guess what? You're already well on your way.

Remember Your "Why"

Take a second and remember why you started all of this. What was it that got you interested in investing? Was it the dream of financial freedom? The desire to quit the 9-to-5 grind and build a life on your terms? Maybe it was about leaving a legacy, or maybe it was just to finally feel *in control* of your money.

Whatever your "why" is, hold onto it. Write it down, stick it on your mirror, or make it the background on your phone. That "why" will be your biggest motivator when things get tough (and they *will* get tough).

The Power of Consistency: Small Wins, Big Impact

You've probably heard it before, but let's hit it again: Consistency is *everything*. No matter how big or small your investments are, showing up consistently is how you build that serious wealth. Here's why:

- **The Snowball Effect**: Every dollar you invest today is like planting a seed. With time, that seed grows, and then it grows some more. Thanks to the magic of *compound interest*, those little investments turn into massive gains over time.

- **Habits Matter**: Building wealth is more about your habits than it is about hitting a home run every time. Make investing a habit. Automate your contributions, set reminders, do whatever it takes to keep that momentum going.

- **Long-Term Vision**: You're in this for the long haul. The ups and downs of the market are just noise when you've got your eyes on the prize. Focus on the bigger picture.

Don't Be Afraid to Keep Learning

Here's the thing: The financial world is always changing. *New trends, new technology,* and *new opportunities* come up all the time. Staying sharp and curious is your secret weapon.

Level Up Your Knowledge

Make it a habit to keep learning. Even if you just read one book a month or listen to a financial podcast on your commute, that constant flow of fresh knowledge keeps you ahead of the game. Remember, *you're the boss* of your money, so keep those skills sharp.

Adapt, but Stay True to Your Plan

Staying informed is one thing, but always jumping to the latest hot trend? That's a recipe for disaster. Stay curious, but keep a steady hand on your overall plan. Flexibility is good; knee-jerk reactions aren't.

The Real Secret? Enjoy the Ride

Yep, you read that right. *Enjoy the process.* Investing isn't all stress and numbers—it's a chance to grow, to learn, and to achieve things you didn't think possible. Celebrate those small wins. Every dollar you earn, every goal you reach, that's progress, and it's worth feeling good about.

Money as a Tool, Not the Goal

At the end of the day, money is just a tool. It's what you can *do* with it that really matters. Maybe it's traveling the world, maybe it's buying your dream home, or maybe it's starting that business you've always dreamed of. Whatever it is, remember: Wealth is there to make life richer in more ways than one.

Stay Balanced, Stay Happy

Keep a balance between living your life now and preparing for tomorrow. Building wealth is amazing, but it's not worth burning out or sacrificing what makes life beautiful. Enjoy the journey, savor the ride, and stay grounded.

Your Final Push: You've Got This

So here's the deal. You're equipped, you're ready, and you're raring to go. The rest is just *showing up and sticking to your guns*. You've got everything you need to crush this journey and build something extraordinary.

- **Trust Yourself**: You know what you're doing. Sure, there's always more to learn, but don't underestimate what you've already achieved.

- **Keep Building**: Every step counts. Every dollar saved, every investment made—it all adds up.
- **Dream Big**: This is *your* financial journey. Set your sights high, keep hustling, and make it happen.

The Beginning of the Rest of Your Life

This isn't just the end of a book; it's the beginning of *your future*. Take a deep breath, give yourself a pat on the back, and go out there and own it. Because guess what? *You've got this*. Now, go out there and keep crushing it.

BONUS SECTIONS

Real-Life Examples from the Big Players: Learning from the Legends

All right, let's dive into the world of some of the most legendary investors of all time! These are the big players, the ones who turned markets on their heads and built fortunes most of us can only imagine. What's cool, though, is that many of them started off not too differently than you or me. They took a few chances, *learned from their mistakes*, and developed strategies that, well, clearly worked out. And here's the best part—each of these stories has lessons you can use in your own journey. So let's take a look at their highs, lows, wins, and yes, some big-time losses too.

Warren Buffett: The King of Consistency

Let's start with the GOAT himself. Warren Buffett, also known as the "Oracle of Omaha," has one of the most impressive track records in investing history. But don't let the old-school vibe fool you; this guy has some serious hustle.

How He Started: Buffett was a bit of a financial prodigy. He bought his first stock at age 11! Yep, you read that right. He didn't start with millions, though. In fact, his first purchase was a humble $114 worth of shares in a company called Cities Service. From that little start, he grew his empire one well-researched choice at a time.

What We Can Learn:

1. **Patience Pays Off**: Buffett's style is all about the long haul. He doesn't freak out over daily market dips. His motto? "Time is the friend of the wonderful business, the enemy of the mediocre."

2. **Stick to Your Guns**: Buffett's famous for not following the crowd. He sticks to what he knows, and he doesn't let hype lead him astray.

Takeaway: Find investments you believe in and let them ride. Don't get caught up in trends if they don't fit your long-term goals.

Ray Dalio: Embracing the Failures

Next up, Ray Dalio, founder of Bridgewater Associates, one of the most successful hedge funds in the world. But Dalio didn't always have it all figured out. In fact, he learned some of his biggest lessons through hard (and expensive) mistakes.

How He Started: Dalio was fascinated by stocks even as a kid. In college, he played around with a few investments, some of which panned out, others… not so much. One of his biggest early mistakes was predicting a stock market crash that never happened, costing him his entire investment. But rather than quit, he dug deeper, researched harder, and developed a "Principles" approach that guides his work.

What We Can Learn:

1. **Failures Are Feedback**: Instead of quitting, Dalio embraced his mistakes and used them as building blocks.
2. **Have a System**: Dalio's method is based on set principles and rules, helping him to stay steady through the ups and downs.

Takeaway: Embrace your mistakes. They're some of the best teachers you'll ever have.

Peter Lynch: The Everyday Investor

Peter Lynch, the man who turned Fidelity's Magellan Fund into one of the most successful mutual funds of all time, has a refreshingly down-to-earth approach to investing.

How He Started: Lynch is famous for saying, "Invest in what you know." He didn't look for fancy, hard-to-understand opportunities. Instead, he invested in businesses he encountered every day. From Dunkin' Donuts to Taco Bell, Lynch looked at what people were buying and based his decisions on what he understood about the market.

What We Can Learn:

1. **Look Around You**: Investment ideas are often right in front of you. If there's a product or service you believe in, look into the company behind it.
2. **Keep It Simple**: You don't have to be a financial genius to make smart investment choices. If you know a good business when you see one, you're already halfway there.

Takeaway: Don't overcomplicate things. Sometimes the best investments are the ones that make the most sense to you.

John Paulson: Timing the Market

Now, this one's a little more complex, but hang with me. John Paulson made billions by betting against the housing market before the 2008 crash. It's a move that's hard to pull off, but Paulson's story is worth knowing about, even if it's more "advanced-level."

How He Started: Paulson was managing a hedge fund and saw signs that the housing market was on shaky ground. His team did the homework and took a major risk, shorting the market in what became known as "The Greatest Trade Ever."

What We Can Learn:

1. **Do Your Research**: Paulson didn't go with his gut—he relied on thorough research.
2. **Sometimes, You Gotta Risk It**: Calculated risks can yield massive rewards, but only if you've got the data to back it up.

Takeaway: High-risk, high-reward moves aren't for everyone, but if you do your research, you might just pull off something amazing.

Oprah Winfrey: Building a Brand

Switching gears from traditional finance to an absolute icon in self-made wealth: Oprah Winfrey. While she's not your classic investor, her approach to building wealth has lessons for anyone.

How She Started: Oprah didn't grow up wealthy. She made her way up in broadcasting, then built her brand from scratch. She invested in herself, her network, and her message—and she never stopped learning.

What We Can Learn:

1. **Invest in Yourself**: Sometimes the best investment is in you. Oprah knew her brand was her biggest asset.
2. **Think Outside the Box**: Wealth isn't always about stocks. Sometimes it's about creating something people value.

Takeaway: Don't be afraid to bet on yourself. Often, the best returns come from what you create.

Elon Musk: Bold Moves, Big Vision

Love him or hate him, Elon Musk is a big player who isn't afraid to take risks. From Tesla to SpaceX, Musk's story is all about pushing the boundaries.

How He Started: Musk didn't start with billions. He made his initial fortune by co-founding PayPal. But instead of chilling with his newfound wealth, he poured it into his next ventures—Tesla and SpaceX.

What We Can Learn:

1. **Think Big**: Musk's approach is about changing the world. He aims high and keeps pushing.
2. **Risk and Reward**: Musk's journey hasn't been easy. He's faced some serious lows, but his willingness to risk it all has led to incredible innovation.

Takeaway: Dream big, and don't be afraid to take risks when you have a vision.

Final Thoughts: The Lessons We Can Use

There you have it—a look at some of the biggest names in the game. These investors all came from different backgrounds, took different paths, and faced different challenges. Yet, *they all share some common traits* that we can take to heart:

- **Be Patient**: Rome wasn't built in a day, and neither is wealth.
- **Learn from Mistakes**: Every failure brings a lesson.
- **Stick to Your Strengths**: Invest in what you know.
- **Keep Growing**: Whether it's new skills or new investments, never stop moving forward.

Real-Life Examples from the Big Players: Learning from the Legends

Each of these legends used their own unique approaches, but at the end of the day, they share one thing: a commitment to the long game. So, take a page from their books, keep hustling, and remember—the journey is just as important as the destination.

Charts and Graphs to Make It Visual: Numbers with Personality

Alright, let's dive into the *visual* side of investing. Now, I know you've been soaking up all the talk about stocks, returns, and financial goals, but seeing those numbers in action? That's a whole new level of understanding. We're going to add some visuals here—*think* easy-to-read charts, graphs, and tables that bring the data to life. So, grab your favorite beverage, settle in, and let's break down what those numbers *really* mean when you see them on paper (or screen).

Why Visuals Matter: The Big Picture at a Glance

Let's be real. Numbers on their own? They can feel like staring at code in the Matrix. That's why charts and graphs are our best buddies here—they take the data and *translate* it into something that just makes sense.

Think of it like this: You're cooking up a recipe for wealth, and these visuals are your measuring cups, timers, and taste tests, all rolled into one. They let you track progress, spot trends, and—most importantly—see how your money's working for you over time.

Tip: Whenever you're evaluating an investment, *always* look for the data visualizations. If you can't find them, ask yourself why. A company that's open and thriving is usually pretty eager to show off its growth numbers.

Growth Over Time: The Classic Line Graph

When it comes to *growth*, the line graph is your best friend. This chart shows you how something (like the stock price of a company or your own investment portfolio) has grown—or shrunk—over time.

Imagine this: You've invested $1,000 in a little-known tech company. It's 2020. Fast forward three years, and you've made annual contributions of $500 while the stock has had its ups and downs. A line graph would show you each of these moves—the dips, the peaks, and everything in between. Here's what we're watching for:

- **Steady Climb**: A smooth, upward slope shows consistent growth.
- **Volatility**: If the line's zigzagging all over, that stock has some *serious mood swings*.
- **Overall Direction**: Even with bumps, if the line trends upward over time, you're looking at growth.

Pro tip: Look for the *10-year line graph* on any investment you're considering. If it's mostly going up? Good sign. If it looks like a roller coaster, buckle up—it's going to be a bumpy ride.

Pie Charts: Breaking Down the Portfolio

Let's talk *diversification*, aka not putting all your eggs in one basket. This is where our buddy, the pie chart, comes in. A pie chart is all about *how your money is divided* among different assets.

Imagine you've got a $10,000 portfolio. Instead of betting it all on one hot tech stock, you've spread it around a bit:

- **40%** in stocks
- **20%** in bonds
- **10%** in real estate
- **15%** in international markets

- **15%** in "fun money"—aka a little for those hot stocks you're experimenting with

By seeing the visual *slices* of this pie, you can spot where you're maybe a little too heavy—or a little too light. If your stock slice looks huge, maybe it's time to add a bit more stability with bonds or real estate.

Takeaway: A balanced pie chart = a balanced portfolio. A tiny sliver in bonds and a big chunk in tech stocks? You're riding on risk.

Bar Graphs: Comparing Like a Pro

Want to see how one investment stacks up against another? *Enter the bar graph.* This type of chart lets you compare values side by side—perfect for spotting winners, losers, and everything in between.

Say you're comparing returns on three different stocks over five years: *Tech Titan, Green Energy Inc., and SteadyBank.* A bar graph could show you:

- How each stock has performed year by year
- Which ones have given you the most growth overall
- And which stocks are... well, just not cutting it

Pro tip: Bar graphs are great for quick checks, but make sure you're not comparing apples to oranges. *Compare companies in the same industry* or investments with similar goals for a clear view.

The Magic of Compound Interest: Visualizing Your Wealth Growth

Ah, compound interest—the sweet, sweet multiplier of money. When you *reinvest your returns*, those returns start earning returns of their own, and that's where the magic really happens.

Here's how a compound interest chart might look:

1. **Year 1-3**: The growth is steady but modest. *You're putting in money, but returns are still just getting warmed up.*
2. **Year 4-7**: Things pick up. Now, your *earnings are starting to earn*, and you're seeing real growth.
3. **Year 8-10 and beyond**: Boom! You're in full-on growth mode now.

Key takeaway: Start early! The longer you're in the game, the bigger that end result. Compound interest is time's best friend.

Risk and Return: The Scatter Plot

Ever wonder if your potential reward is worth the risk? *Scatter plots* can help answer that. By plotting different investments based on their level of risk (on one axis) and their potential return (on the other), you get a visual of where each option sits.

Imagine it like a treasure map:

- **Top-right quadrant**: High-risk, high-return (think tech startups or cryptocurrency)
- **Bottom-left quadrant**: Low-risk, low-return (more like treasury bonds or savings accounts)
- **Middle ground**: That sweet spot between risk and return

Scatter plots give you a bird's-eye view of *what you're getting into*. This is a tool that can really help when you're adding a new investment and wondering, *"Is this worth the risk?"*

Reality check: Most people should have a nice mix, with only a few investments sitting in that risky high-return zone. After all, it's about balance.

Table Time: Let's Get Detailed

Charts and graphs are awesome, but sometimes you need the *nitty-gritty details*. That's where tables come in handy. Tables let you line up data points side-by-side, making it easy to spot patterns or outliers.

Here's how tables come to the rescue:

- **Comparing Funds**: Want to see expense ratios, returns, and risk levels for a few mutual funds? A table lays it all out.
- **Tracking Progress**: Tables can track your monthly or yearly investment contributions, showing you exactly how you're pacing toward your goals.
- **Analyzing Costs**: Costs eat into profits, so a table that breaks down each fee—brokerage, fund, etc.—is your best friend.

Hot tip: When looking at investment options, pay attention to the *expense ratio*. Even a small percentage point difference can add up over time.

The Big Picture: How It All Comes Together

By now, you're equipped with a visual toolbox to turn all that investment lingo into clear, easy-to-understand pictures. The key to winning this game? *Use your tools*. These charts, graphs, and tables aren't just for looks—they're your roadmaps, your guides, your "aha!" moments waiting to happen.

1. **Find the Tools**: Always look for these visuals on company websites, brokerage platforms, and in annual reports.
2. **Interpret Like a Pro**: The more you use them, the faster you'll spot trends and patterns.
3. **Make Informed Choices**: Let these charts and graphs guide your decisions, because numbers don't lie.

Glossary of Terms: Because Who Doesn't Love a Cheat Sheet?

Alright, you've waded through all the jargon, and now it's time for a little help. Here's a glossary, not your typical boring one though—we'll keep it lively so these words stick. Picture this as your very own *financial survival kit,* a pocket guide to decode the lingo, so you can keep up with the best of them. Because, hey, we all need a little refresher sometimes.

A

Asset
An asset is *anything you own that has value.* Your house? Asset. Stocks? Asset. Even that rare comic book collection you're hoping will sell big someday? Yep, asset. Assets are your personal treasures, the things that add to your wealth. *In investing, the more assets, the merrier.*

B

Bear Market
Imagine the stock market is a grizzly bear—big, kind of intimidating, and...it's *falling asleep.* A bear market is when stock prices are on a steady decline, usually by 20% or more. People feel nervous, like they're huddling around a campfire trying to keep warm while the "bear" hangs out in the distance.

Bull Market
Now, picture that same grizzly bear waking up, stretching, and deciding it's time to run. A bull market is when prices are rising and investors are feeling excited, like the sun's shining, and everyone's got high hopes for their

investments. Bulls are aggressive and fast—a perfect metaphor for a market that's growing strong.

Blue Chip Stock
These are the *VIP stocks,* the ones everyone wants to own. Blue chip stocks are shares in massive, stable companies that have been around forever, like Apple or Coca-Cola. They're reliable, they're high quality, and they're the stocks that make investors feel safe when things get bumpy.

C

Capital
The money you bring to the table. Capital is *cash for investments,* plain and simple. It's what you put in at the start to make something bigger—like the cash you use to start a business or buy stocks.

Compound Interest
Alright, this is where things get magical. Compound interest is when *the interest you earn starts earning interest on itself.* Your money is out there making money on top of money. Think of it as a little snowball that you roll down a mountain. It gets bigger and bigger, and by the time it reaches the bottom, it's huge. Compound interest works the same way with your investments.

Cryptocurrency
Digital money for the tech-savvy. Cryptocurrency, like Bitcoin or Ethereum, is *virtual cash* that's not backed by any government or central bank. It's wild, it's unregulated, and for some investors, it's the future of money.

D

Diversification
This is fancy talk for *not putting all your eggs in one basket.*

Glossary of Terms: Because Who Doesn't Love a Cheat Sheet?

Diversification means spreading out your investments so if one thing goes bad, the whole plan doesn't crash and burn. It's like a buffet of stocks, bonds, and real estate that balances each other out.

Dividend
Dividends are *like little thank-you notes from the companies you invest in*. When a company does well, they may share some of their profits with you, the shareholder, in the form of cash or extra shares. It's their way of saying, "Thanks for believing in us!"

E

Equity
Equity is your ownership stake in a company or asset. If you own a chunk of a business, that's equity. Think of it as your *slice of the pie*. The more equity you have, the bigger your slice (and hopefully, your profits).

Exchange-Traded Fund (ETF)
An ETF is like a *basket of goodies*—stocks, bonds, or other assets—that you can buy and sell like a stock. It's diversified, it's flexible, and it's often cheaper than buying individual stocks. A smart way to invest without betting on a single horse.

F

Financial Advisor
Your money coach. A financial advisor helps you figure out how to make the most of your cash, whether it's retirement planning or managing investments. Find a good one, and they'll be worth every penny.

Fiscal Year
A fiscal year is a company's *budget year*, which doesn't

Glossary of Terms: Because Who Doesn't Love a Cheat Sheet?

always match the calendar year. It's the 12-month period they use to plan, report earnings, and track their financial health.

G

Growth Stock
A growth stock is one of those fast-moving, high-energy investments. These are shares in companies expected to grow quickly, often reinvesting profits to fuel even more growth. They're exciting, but they also come with a riskier ride.

I

Index Fund
This is a *group of stocks* that represents a market index, like the S&P 500. It's a way to invest in a whole bunch of companies at once, often at a low cost. Great for beginners who want to play it safe and get a taste of the whole market pie.

Inflation
Inflation is the *slow, steady rise in prices* over time. It means your money buys a little less every year, which is why investing is key to keeping your buying power strong.

M

Mutual Fund
A mutual fund is a *pool of money* that investors put together, managed by a professional who decides which stocks or bonds to buy. It's a simple way to diversify without picking each investment yourself.

Glossary of Terms: Because Who Doesn't Love a Cheat Sheet?

P

Portfolio
A portfolio is *your collection of investments,* like your own little art gallery of financial assets. It could be a mix of stocks, bonds, real estate, and maybe a sprinkle of crypto—whatever assets you've gathered up to reach your financial goals.

Principal
The original sum of money you put into an investment, the *core amount* you're starting with. You want to keep this safe, while making it grow over time.

R

Rate of Return
This is the percentage gain (or loss) you see on an investment. Rate of return is *your scorecard,* showing how much your money has grown or shrunk.

Real Estate Investment Trust (REIT)
A REIT is a company that owns, operates, or finances income-producing real estate. It's a way to invest in real estate *without buying property yourself.*

S

Stock
A share in a company. Owning stock means you own *a piece of the business,* no matter how small. Stocks can go up, down, and sideways, but over time, they're the key to building wealth.

Stock Market
This is the place where stocks get bought and sold. The stock market is like *a giant online store for investments,* with

Glossary of Terms: Because Who Doesn't Love a Cheat Sheet?

people all over the world buying and selling shares in businesses big and small.

T

Tax-Deferred
This means you're not paying taxes on an investment until later. Tax-deferred accounts, like some retirement accounts, let your money grow *tax-free for now*, with Uncle Sam taking his cut when you cash out.

Treasury Bond
This is a loan to the U.S. government. Treasury bonds are *super safe investments,* but they usually offer lower returns because the risk of Uncle Sam not paying up is...well, low.

V

Volatility
Volatility is the measure of *how much an investment goes up and down.* A stock with high volatility is all over the place; low volatility means it's a pretty stable ride.

Y

Yield
This is how much income an investment pays you, usually as a percentage of its cost. Yield is like your *bonus check* for holding onto an investment, showing how much bang you're getting for your buck.

W

Wealth
Your stash, your nest egg, your empire. Wealth is *all the*

Glossary of Terms: Because Who Doesn't Love a Cheat Sheet?

money and assets you've built up over time, thanks to saving, investing, and maybe a little luck.

There you go—your cheat sheet to keep you feeling confident and in control. Keep this glossary close; every time you hear someone throw around a fancy term, you'll know exactly what they mean.

X

Expense Ratio
The *annual fee charged by an investment fund,* such as an ETF or mutual fund, expressed as a percentage of your total investment. Think of it as the cost of keeping your money managed. Lower is better since high fees can chip away at your returns over time.

Z

Zero-Coupon Bond
A bond that *doesn't pay regular interest* like most bonds. Instead, you buy it at a discount, and when it matures, you get the full face value. It's a "pay me later" setup that can be ideal if you're saving for something specific in the future, like retirement.

Glossary of Terms: Because Who Doesn't Love a Cheat Sheet?

There it is, your *ultimate cheat sheet*. Each of these terms is a building block, a stepping stone to navigating the sometimes wild world of finance and investing. Understanding the language of investing puts you in the driver's seat, helping you make smarter moves with your money. Keep this guide in your back pocket, because the more you know, the further you'll go.

Exercises to Sharpen Your Skills: Keep the Momentum Rolling

Alright, so you've read through the book, laughed, cringed, and maybe even felt that *light bulb moment*. But here's the thing—*real learning* kicks in when you roll up your sleeves and get some hands-on practice. So, let's get into some exercises that'll help cement all this investment knowledge, keep you sharp, and give you that confidence boost every time you hear the word "market."

Each of these exercises is designed to be easy to dive into without needing a PhD in finance, but if you do each one, you'll be that much closer to *investment guru status*. Ready? Let's get those gears turning!

1. Personal Budget Breakdown: Your Money, Visualized

Objective: Break down your income and spending into clear categories and see where your money is going.

Steps:

- Pull out your latest bank and credit card statements.
- Identify three main categories: **Essentials** (rent, bills), **Wants** (eating out, subscriptions), and **Savings/Investments** (retirement, brokerage account).
- Calculate what percentage of your income each category takes up.

Reflection: Now, *think* about what you're seeing. Are you spending more on streaming services than you thought? Maybe that's money that could go into investments. Adjust as you see fit, even if it's just a little. Remember, *investing is a mindset,* not just numbers on a spreadsheet.

2. Stock Shopping Spree: Mock Portfolio Setup

Objective: Start building a sample portfolio to get familiar with researching stocks without spending a dime.

Steps:

- Pick **five companies** you're interested in. Could be anything from tech giants to your favorite coffee shop's parent company.
- Research their **financials** (look at their revenue, earnings, stock price history) and **business model** (what do they actually do?).
- Create a mock portfolio by "buying" a set number of shares (use sites like Yahoo Finance or MarketWatch to see real-time prices).

Reflection: Track your "portfolio" over a month. Did they go up or down? What factors influenced them? How did it make you feel to see them fluctuate? The more you familiarize yourself, the better you'll get at spotting trends, staying calm, and planning long-term.

3. Play the "What's Their P/E Ratio?" Game

Objective: Practice finding and understanding Price-to-Earnings (P/E) ratios to measure a stock's value.

Steps:

- Choose **three stocks** you've heard of.
- Look up each stock's P/E ratio and jot it down.
- Research what the *average P/E ratio* is in their industry to see if they're overvalued, undervalued, or on par.

Reflection: This little exercise gives you a feel for evaluating whether a stock is a "good deal" compared to others in its sector. If one of them has a high P/E ratio, think about why investors might still buy in—do they expect massive growth? This is just another way to build that intuition.

4. Investment Goals Vision Board

Objective: Visualize what you're working towards, and make it real.

Steps:

- Grab a sheet of paper (or make it fancy with a digital collage).
- Map out your *short-term, mid-term,* and *long-term* goals—anything from "save $5k for a vacation" to "retire comfortably at 60."
- Think of what investment steps will support each goal. Does your short-term goal need a safe, low-risk fund? Could your long-term goals be backed by higher-growth stock investments?

Reflection: Hang it somewhere you'll see it. This isn't just a Pinterest exercise; it's about *connecting your goals to real actions.* Revisit it every so often to track progress and re-inspire yourself.

5. Read the Financial News with Purpose

Objective: Cultivate a habit of daily news-checking with an investor's eye.

Steps:

- Pick one financial news source (e.g., CNBC, Bloomberg, Yahoo Finance).

- Choose a **headline** and dive into the article.
- Ask yourself, "How does this news affect the market?" and then ask, "Would this news affect how I invest in this company?"

Reflection: Notice patterns. Do you see repeated themes, like inflation fears or tech trends? The news can give you hints about how big players think. It's like getting a backstage pass to the market's pulse.

---

6. Price Movement Detective

Objective: Analyze price movements to understand how stock prices change daily.

Steps:

- Track the daily price of a single stock (say, one of your mock portfolio picks) for a month.
- Each day, note the **high, low, and closing prices** and anything notable happening with the company or market.

Reflection: Over time, you'll start seeing patterns—when a company's earnings report comes out, the stock might jump or dip. Or maybe market trends affect certain sectors at the same time. *Spotting these patterns will make you more intuitive* as an investor.

---

7. Earnings Report Deep Dive

Objective: Learn how to read an earnings report without getting lost in the financial lingo.

Steps:

- Choose one company's earnings report (usually released quarterly).
- Look up **net income, revenue, earnings per share (EPS)**, and any *guidance* for future quarters.
- Write down what these numbers mean in plain English. Is the company growing? Are they making more profit per share?

Reflection: These reports are a company's "report card," showing how they performed. Getting comfortable with them gives you the power to know whether a company's moving in the right direction—or if it's time to bail.

8. Debt-to-Income Ratio Check (On Yourself!)

Objective: Understand your own financial health the same way analysts look at companies.

Steps:

- Calculate your **monthly income** and your **monthly debts** (loans, credit card payments, etc.).
- Divide your monthly debt by your monthly income to get your debt-to-income ratio.

Reflection: If it's high, that's okay; you just know it's an area to focus on. *Just like a company's balance sheet,* you want to ensure you're in a healthy spot with manageable debt, so you're ready to start investing more.

9. Create a Risk Tolerance Chart

Objective: Identify your risk tolerance to better understand where you should invest.

Steps:

- List out different types of investments (bonds, stocks, mutual funds, ETFs, etc.).
- Rate each on a scale of 1-10 based on your comfort level with their risk (1 = very comfortable, 10 = no thanks).
- Take note of where you land with higher-risk investments.

Reflection: Knowing your personal *risk tolerance* helps you invest confidently. If you're risk-averse, it's cool to play it safe. If you've got the guts for high risk, then it's all about channeling that into the right stocks.

---

10. Real-Life Money Mentor Outreach

Objective: Connect with someone who's been there, done that, and learn from their experience.

Steps:

- Identify someone in your network or a professional who's experienced in investing.
- Ask if you can take them for coffee or a virtual chat to ask about their *biggest wins and lessons learned*.

Reflection: Real-life wisdom trumps textbook knowledge any day. They might share tips and mistakes that'll help you skip some beginner errors and put you on the right track faster.

www.ingramcontent.com/pod-product-compliance
Lightning Source LLC
Chambersburg PA
CBHW031618210526
45464CB00004B/1636